The Twenty-Five
Unbelievable Years
1945 - 1969

RALPH D. WINTER

THE TWENTY-FIVE

UNBELIEVABLE YEARS

1945 to 1969

William Carey Library

CHRISTIAN MISSION BOOKS

South Pasadena, California

International Standard Book Number: 0-87808-102-X
Library of Congress Catalog Number: 73-1254459

Seventh Printing

Published by the William Carey Library
533 Hermosa Street
South Pasadena, Calif. 91030
Telephone 213-682-2047

PRINTED IN THE UNITED STATES OF AMERICA

Contents

FIGURES 7
PREFACE 9

1 THE RETREAT OF THE WEST 11

The Official End to Political Imperialism 13
Heightened Economic Imperialism 14
Nationalistic Imperialism 15
Mixed Attitudes 15
Cultural Imperialism 16
Political Boundaries and Cultural Minorities 16
The Technological Explosion 19
The Psychological Impact 19

2 THE FATE OF THE YOUNGER CHURCHES 21

The Emergence of the National Church 22
The Indigenous Church 23
The Evidences of a Major Movement 27
The Younger Churches and the Ecumenical Movement 29
The Theological Problem of Diversity 31

3 THE FATE OF CHRISTIANITY 36

Communism and Christianity 37
The Impression of a Dwindling Movement 40
Christianity in a World Demanding Change 42

4 THE FATE OF THE MISSIONS 47

The Cutting of Roots 47
The Closing of Doors 48
The Deepening Pessimism 49
The Unbelievable Record 51
The Turmoil in Mission Theory 57
From Missions to Mission? 62
The Councils and the Congresses 64
Church, Mission, and the Oikoumene 67

5 PREPARATION FOR TOMORROW 74

The Shape of Tomorrow 75
Structure as Servant or Master? 77
Strategic Consultation 79
What is the Goal? 82

APPENDIX: THE MAN AND THE ISSUE 85

A. *The Reluctant Missionary 86*
B. *The Tapestry of the Christian Story 93*
C. *The Anatomy of the Christian Mission 97*

REFERENCE NOTES 113

Figures

1   THE RETREAT OF THE WEST   12

2   THE NEW NATIONS   12

3   GROWTH IN PERSONNEL OVERSEAS   53
     OF SELECTED MISSION AGENCIES

4   PROTESTANT FOREIGN MISSIONARY   54
     PERSONNEL

5   COMPARATIVE STATISTICS OF OVERSEAS   54
     MISSIONARY FORCES

6   GROWTH IN INCOME, 1960-1968   56

7   GROWTH IN PERSONNEL, 1946-1969   56

8   ATTENDANCE, INTER-VARSITY   56
     MISSIONARY CONVENTIONS

9   SELECTED BOOKS BY LATOURETTE   92

10   A COMPARISON OF LATOURETTE'S   95
     TWO MAJOR WORKS

Preface

It has been an exciting task to try to sum up the events standing immediately behind us, and in so doing to discover, first, that the past twenty-five years constitute a massive historical transition that is as foreboding as it is unique in the past 1500 years; then to measure the fortune of the worldwide Christian movement throughout this period and to discover, secondly, the astonishing fact that in an hour of gloom on every side, when church rolls and giving are sagging, and crime and immorality are ballooning, that Christianity, as a movement, was never in better shape.

But this is not merely an isolated attempt to discuss the past twenty-five years. The many references throughout this essay to the late Kenneth Scott Latourette make clear that this is a conscious attempt to continue on from the point, 1944, where his work A History of the Expansion of Christianity leaves off. But we would not merely start there and work self-sufficiently from that point on. These pages could not, if they tried, be totally independent of his many other writings. For this reason the first two items in the appendix will introduce the reader both to the man and his other significant books which were written both before and during the period under discussion, even though in none of them did he attempt to sum up these twenty-five years as a period.

While we could not attempt to imitate his style, much less repeat all the materials in his other writings on this period, we do hope to have written with his same fact-based, optimistic perspective, and to have done so in one sense especially. One of the unusual elements in Latourette's perspective was his desire to go beyond mere Church history and to describe what may be called the infra-structure of the Christian movement---that is, to describe Christianity as a movement which is more (but not less) than an account of the rise and development of the various churchly structures. Since this matter of infra-structure is a crucial issue at this time of the wholesale rethinking of the Christian cause and its structure, we have appended a third item, a short article entitle "The Anatomy of the Christian Mission," which puts this issue in a larger context.

The whole purpose of this study is to offer hope and insight to students, laymen, pastors and even missionaries. There is nothing honorable about a pessimism that is unwarranted. Such pessimism is a poison that can pollute the environment. It can pervert industries, nations, churches, and young people's minds. A British visitor in the U. S. recently observed that Americans have been overtaken by a fit of compulsive pessimism. Everything is assumed to be going wrong on both foreign and domestic fronts. Newspapers daily add a new load of gloom. Christians, whose hopes encompass the world, are offered little for rejoicing.

Yet on the home front there is eminent reason for hope. In eight years the number of people listed as living in poverty has dropped from 22% to 13%, and the number of black families earning more than $15,000 per year has gone from 20,000 to 400,000. Is this hopeless? Or when Christians think of Asia as impenetrable do they forget that in the city of Seoul, Korea alone there are now 600 Christian churches? But let us not anticipate the text.

Latourette cannot be blamed for any of the specific conclusions in this essay, although whatever virtues it has are no doubt to be attributed either to him or to the many friends who have read this in manuscript and have made many specific suggestions. They too must be unblamed though not unnamed: David Barrett, Dale Brunner, Raymond Buker, Sr., Harry Burke, Clyde Cook, Harold Cook, Ralph Covell, Edward Dayton, Arthur Glasser, Harold Lindsell, John A. Mackay, Donald McGavran, Robert Munger, George Peters, Paul Rees, Alan Tippett, and Peter Wagner. My wife's collaboration has been on a scale that sets her apart from all others.

1

THE RETREAT

OF THE WEST

No matter how you look at it, the story of the white man's four-hundred-year conquest of all other men is fantastic. It is a story of traders, soldiers, diplomats, and missionaries, of good men and bad, of meanness and high-mindedness. But however it was accomplished, four hundred years of political expansion were rolled back to zero in just twenty-five years.

These unbelievable years began with the hideous mushroom cloud above Hiroshima on August 6, 1945. They ended twenty-five years later (lacking twenty-one days), when man put his foot down on the surface of the earth's moon. But these convenient boundary markers do not define the uniqueness of this period. During this period, after centuries of empire building, the political power of the Western cultural tradition reached its nadir and exploded in a vast worldwide display of fireworks in the permanent embarrassment of history's greatest war. With this internal weakness displayed for all to see, the year 1945 opened a new period in which the European colonial empire began to retreat. The destructive power of the hydrogen bomb brought many to the conclusion that never again could the West afford a massive internal struggle, but this uneasy cold-war peace came too late to prevent the loss of the non-Western world.

The new era was marked by perennial international tension and continued exorbitant military expense, yet it encompassed incredible economic miracles, not only in Japan and Germany, but elsewhere. Following so closely upon bitter enmity, the emergence of a European Common Market seemed

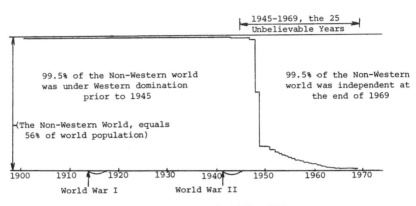

Figure 1: THE RETREAT OF THE WEST

THE WEST RELEASES ITS POLITICAL GRIP ON THE NON-WESTERN WORLD

Date of Independence	Per Cent of Non-Western World	Name of New Nations
1943-45	.5	Lebanon, Syria, Iceland
1946-49	82.4	Jordan, Philippines, Pakistan, India (Japan), Burma, Ceylon, N.Korea, Israel, S. Korea, Laos, (People's China), Cambodia, Indonesia
1950-55	3.4	Libya, N. Vietnam, S. Vietnam, (Egypt)
1956-60	9.3	Sudan, Morocco, Tunisia, Ghana, Malaysia, Guinea, Cameroon, Togo, Malagasy, Congo-Kinshasa, Somalia, Dahomey, Niger, Upper Volta, Ivory Coast, Chad, Central African Republic, Congo-Braz., Cyprus,, Gabon, Senegal, Mali, Nigeria, Mauritania
1961-65	3.6	Sierra Leone, Kuwait, Tanzania, Western Samoa, Burundi, Ruanda, Algeria, Jamaica, Trinidad & Tobago, Uganda, Kenya, Malawi, Malta, Zambia, Gambia, Maldive Islands, Singapore
1966-69	.3	Guyana, Botswana, Lesotho, Barbados, So. Yemen, Nauru, Mauritius, Swaziland, Equatorial Guinea

Figure 2: THE NEW NATIONS

unbelievable. The cybernetic age, the industrial and scientific feat of the moon landings, and the holocausts of riot and ghetto fires in major U.S. cities would all have seemed equally unbelievable if foreseen in the forties. Despite new and flashing insights into man's unbelievable potential, pessimism and increasing cynicism clouded the age. Optimism was expressed only when carefully hedged about with qualifications deriving from new and deeper doubts about man's very nature.

Yet, while all these things characterized the "Unbelievable Twenty-Five Years," they did not precisely define the 1945-69 limits. Those limits result from the purely quantitative fact that 1945 was virtually the beginning of a transition of which 1969 was virtually the end, the end of Western political imperialism.

The Official End to Political Imperialism

The most obvious outward trait of our twenty-five-year period was the unprecedented "Retreat of the West." Few in 1944 were prepared for the suddenness of the collapse of four hundred years of European empire building in the non-Western world. Yet this collapse was documented by the fascinating and awesome story told indirectly by the cumulative record of the new nations which joined the United Nations. Almost every time a new nation stepped forward, it meant a step backward for some colonial empire. Figure 1 shows the result of a centuries-long build-up of Western political domination over the peoples of the earth and the massive, precipitous reversal of that trend. The largest ethnic unit to shake off European domination was the Chinese, although early in 1970 it was not registered on the rolls of the United Nations.[1] The table in Figure 2 gives the data plotted in Figure 1.

The physical dimensions of the Retreat of the West are apparent from the graph and the table. Yet many meaningful dimensions of the period cannot be as easily measured numerically. The end of political colonialism was only one aspect of the whole, though it was the most obvious. Some people, perhaps many early in the period, supposed that the political withdrawal alone was the very definition of freedom. It is unquestionable that the withdrawal of colonial power was a necessary if not sufficient condition of true freedom.

Nevertheless, great anticipations of freedom were compromised since, as we shall see, there is an element of imperialism in any continued force that takes initiative from indigenous national leadership, no matter how beneficial that force might be in a material sense.

Heightened Economic Imperialism

Thus a factor tending to counterbalance the withdrawal of political imperialism was a heightened economic imperialism. The impinging of Western industrial and business enterprises upon the non-Western peoples generally increased. Sukarno warned of this in 1955 at Bandung:

Colonialism also has its modern dress in the form of economic control, intellectual control, and actual physical control by a small but alien community within a nation. Wherever, whenever and however it appears, colonialism is an evil thing and one which must be eradicated from the earth![2]

Indeed, in some cases the withdrawal of the colonial governments gave a freer reign to Western business enterprises than was the case prior to independence. Sometimes a new nationalist government was less able or less willing to protect certain elements of the population than was the former colonial government. Thus, a kind of economic imperialism continued despite the decrease in political imperialism. Ironically, the colonial apparatus had often been established in the first place in order to protect the non-Western peoples from the impact of unregulated Western business interests. But the tendency of man to dominate man is not easily eliminated whether the government is colonial or not. And, if some foreign private firms mistreated local peoples, national private firms were also guilty of the same. One source of misunderstanding arose from the fact that governments of the new nations often exerted far more control over private enterprises than did Western governments (particularly that of the United States). Thus the U.S. government itself was most often blamed for harmful commercial influences. The scope of continuing economic imperialism was inevitably widened by the enormously increased industrial power of the Western heartland in Europe and America.

Nationalistic Imperialism

A third dimension of the period was the uneven character of the new nationalist governments, and the evidence of what might be called local nationalistic imperialism. Westerners sometimes evaluated the new governments merely in terms of their friendliness or neutrality in relation to the communist-capitalist polarization within the West itself, ignoring the quality of the relation of that government to its own people. Many a sub-population found itself subject to greater tyranny under a new nationalistic regime than under the former colonial rule.

Mixed Attitudes

A fourth feature of the period was the curious and paradoxical mixture of attitudes of non-Westerners toward former colonial powers. Any generalization along these lines would be only partially true, but often it appeared that the newly independent people stridently condemned their former colonial masters while maintaining a certain respect and admiration for their culture and their peoples. New nations formerly under British domination might be anti-British, but they shared even less affection for other Europeans. The Indonesians switched to English in university classes in the early days of their independence, while the Indians tried to exclude English, and for the same reasons. But by early 1970 the Indians had long sensed that the British were their most understanding friends; and in Indonesia a rebirth of friendliness toward the Dutch had appeared. Curiously, the newly-liberated peoples tended to look upon their former masters with mixed hatred and respect while the colonial powers tended to look at their former subjects with a condescension mixed with both pride and concern. These contrasts were not merely found in different elements in the populations involved, but were combined in a paradoxical way in the hearts of single individuals. This explains why extremist attitudes often represented simplistic and false perspectives.

Cultural Imperialism

In view of this complexity, it is not surprising to note that there was a lingering, indeed increasing, cultural imperialism. The withdrawal of political power often signaled a return to national languages and cultural ways. Ironically, however, in many cases the newly independent peoples immediately adopted previously unacceptable elements of the former conquering culture, now that political resistance was unnecessary. Continuing economic imperialism brought a continuing flood of foreign merchandise, periodicals, and related customs. In an attempt to feel equal to the former colonial culture, local national governments often dictated crash programs of face lifting for capital cities, new superhighways, Western style schools, and even Western dress. The Tanzanian government, for example, found itself attempting to outlaw the Masai traditional costume by imposing fines on Masai men not wearing trousers: this the colonial government never did. Some governments would have needed an income twenty times as large in order to provide Western style public school facilities for all children through twelfth grade. Such governments failed to realize that the U.S. educational system followed upon a long process of slowly developed technological power, and that such a pattern might not be the best immediate move for a developing nation. A well-known radical priest, Ivan Illich, made persuasive claims that a limited public school system of a showcase variety---which was all most non-Western nations could afford---only served to defend the status quo of the wealthy by merely offering the masses a feeling of inferiority to go with their poverty. Thus in spite of political freedom, the continuing existence of largely unintended cultural imperialism made it next to impossible for the new nations to pursue indigenous cultural goals unhampered by external influence.

Political Boundaries and Cultural Minorities

An even more problematic legacy from the colonial era was the vast system of apparently indelible marks that constituted the often illogical boundaries of the new nations. Even in Europe boundaries had long been a problem; years

earlier H. G. Wells had proposed a re-drawings of the map
in order to avoid the disruption of ethnic and cultural en-
tities. But much more serious was what happened in Africa,
where political boundaries sliced in two (or more) pieces
approximately one-third of all the indigenous tribal peoples.
But whether it happened in Europe or in Africa---whether it
was the Basque nation cut in two by the border between
France and Spain, or the Masai nation split by the Kenya-
Tanzania border---the effect was to postpone or perhaps
permanently deny the maximum development of the legitimate
aspirations for self-determination of such nations. Yet even
supposing that the colonists could have adjusted the boundaries before they left, so as not to split any one people between
two countries, this would still not have assured the self-
determination of any one group. The new nations were almost always what could be called "composite" nations,
gathering together many totally separate peoples into a
single political entity. Obviously no one tribe could successfully go on its own way, but the colonial legacy, in demon-
strating the economic advantage of unity across a large
area, did not successfully propose or develop the kind of
diversity-within-unity in the governmental structure that
could enable minorities to escape the local tyranny of a
totalitarian nationalism.

One reason the colonial powers failed to implant the kind
of government that would allow healthy ethnic diversity within an overall, benign political unity was that few colonial
powers had achieved that kind of government back home.
The Basques, who continued to struggle throughout the entire
period of the Retreat, seeking independence from both French
and Spanish central governments; the Bretons, whose de-
mands for decentralization pushed De Gaulle into a position
which contributed to his political downfall; the 700,000 Welsh-
speaking Celts, who still fondly recalled the year 1284 when
last a Welshman was the Prince of Wales; the twenty million
Blacks in the United States who grasped for power in order
to gain the measure of freedom and self-determination which
was their due; the American Indians, who in 1969 dramati-
cally seized the island of Alcatraz as a step toward the recog-
nition of their rights; the twelve million Spanish-speaking
Americans in the United States, for whom in 1969 a public

school was established in which for the first time their
language was treated as a permanent, not temporary, phenomenon in American culture; the Czechs, imprisoned in
their own land; the two hundred linguistic minorities within
Russia proper---all these minorities and many hundreds of
others in almost every nation of the world represented in
1970 a monstrous, urgent, yet unresolved problem. The
withdrawal of colonialism brought the wider problem into
prominence. Thus, the decision of the British to allow the
Burmese to chart their own national course was an example
to the Burmese: could they allow the Karens the same type
of self-determination within Burma? It was a portent to the
British themselves: could they look at the Scottish and Welsh
within the United Kingdom with the same new perspective
they had applied in a distant land?

It was thus clear that the period of the Retreat of the
West was pregnant with profound meaning, not merely a
shift in the balance of political power. It seemed that almost
all secular problems were secondary to the complex phenomenon of the growth and development of a people, and modern
man was forced more than ever to come to grips with it.
It was as though a gardener lifted up the stones and bricks
that had fallen on top of many different plants, hoping to see
those little plants rise into newly available air and light to
develop the true potential of their genes. But how could
that be accomplished in the case of a group of people?
Classically, the Roman Empire sought to "save" conquered
peoples by Latinizing them, and through many centuries the
religious imperialism inherent in the exclusive use of the
Latin language in the Roman Catholic mass implied a strategy
of unity-through-uniformity. The colonial powers of modern
times generally allowed self-determination with far greater
enlightenment than did old Rome, but by the 1960's contemporary insights into the intrinsic value in disparate cultures
made all colonial plans for self-determination to be clumsy
approximations of an ideal. Thus it was that the surging new
role of the many minority cultures became a prominent and
unprecedented development within the overall phenomenon of
the Retreat of the West.

The Technological Explosion

The unprecedented surge of Western technology, which reached even into the new nations, was another phenomenon which tended to counterbalance the sense of overall retreat in this period. In one sense World War II was a contest of technological powers. On both sides of the conflict the contribution of science and industry to war was more significant and spectacular than at any time in history. In the development of atomic weapons and of radar, for example, the scientists themselves seemed to be on the front lines of the conflict. The direct results of the war left Europe and Japan temporarily crippled, while the United States remained standing on her feet. But the rapid recovery of Germany and Japan showed that both sides were able to profit from war-developed technological gains. In this sense the war was a vast, disciplined schooling for Western society in science and technology. Both systems engineering and the cybernetic revolution had their roots in the war. Futhermore, the people of the United States gained a new sense of world affairs simply as a result of sending millions of men to the far corners of the earth. It was as though the whole nation had been sent back to school to study world political geography. One result of this was that the impact of the technological revolution in the West was greatly multiplied as thousands of business and industrial contacts in the non-Western world were forged by American servicemen in tours of duty on foreign soil.

The Psychological Impact

Despite all the factors we have listed that indicated the heightened influence of Western civilization, the period nevertheless witnessed a profound change in the psychology and outlook of the people of the Western world. The flood of Dutchmen who inundated the Low Countries in their retreat from Indonesia was in a physical way no more traumatic than the cumulative psychological shock produced by the Retreat of the West in the minds and hearts of millions of thinking people in other Western nations. Major cities of Europe lay in ruins. Millions of displaced persons had to be reassimilated. The United States, while it entered into the Marshall Plan with great energy and with great expenditure of funds, did not suffer physically to any comparable extent. Even its loss of men in action was relatively light. Yet in America as well as in Europe immense pessimism dominated the thinking and the planning of leaders, both secular and Christian. Theologians like Reinhold Niebuhr led the way in demolishing earlier idealistic hopes for man. Thousands of American missionaries forced out of China carried with them a deep sense of the failure of Christian efforts in China. Missionary statesmen at Willingen in 1952 felt that Christians might well be prepared for a long period of reversal and defeat in the expansion of Christianity in the non-Western world.

Thus, as we conclude this sketch of the Retreat of the West, we acknowledge that it had both direct and indirect significance. On the one hand it is true that the pressure of the West on the non-West was in many ways greater than ever at the end of the period. Yet on the other hand, in early 1970 it seemed as though no Western nation would ever again venture forth to take charge of a non-Western territory, nor even to commit military forces in a land war against a non-Western nation. This fact affected the thinking of people to the point that our sectional titles have been chosen simply to make contact with the mind-set of the average reader in early 1970. Thus we enquire anxiously about the fate of the younger churches, approaching the subject from the perspective of the Retreat as though we must at least begin by assuming that their situation was bleak and gloomy. We must even speak of the fate of Christianity itself within the mood of the period. In the same vein, we must speak of the fate of the missions, since most readers would have supposed that surely the mission apparatus would crumble along with the Western colonial administrations. Yet, as we have already seen, the period of the Retreat was very complex, involving many elements which were the striking opposite of retreat. There were, in fact, so many vital, new factors favorable to the expansion of Christianity that the period rightly understood might better have been treated in an optimistic light. Not our titles but our data must tell the true story of the unbelievable twenty-five years.

2

THE FATE OF

THE YOUNGER CHURCHES

Toward the end of World War II, Henry Pitney Van Dusen compiled a little book consisting primarily of excerpts from letters written home to the United States by American servicemen in the Pacific. Entitled They Found the Church There,[3] it portrayed the servicemen's amazement and grateful surprise when in countless instances, due to the solid existence of the Christian church in the Pacific Islands, former cannibals greeted them with friendship and trust. At a time when some American cities registered only 6 percent church membership, it is understandable that these servicemen would be astonished to discover that well over half of all the people in Oceania were members of Christian churches.

A similar surprise resulted in 1960 when the Belgian colonial apparatus withdrew from the Congo. Chaos reigned. Two thousand missionaries were flown out. Newspapers recounted for weeks on end the collapse of the white man's house of cards, and predicted a return to the Dark Ages for the heart of Africa. The effect of this upon Christians, even missionaries, was predictable. One lay promoter of a Christian radio station situated two thousand miles to the west of the Congo pleaded for greater support on the basis that radio waves were now to be the only Christian influence reaching into the Congo. But the fact was that by 1960 there were in the Congo itself well over ten thousand churches of Protestant origin alone, whose membership comprised fully one-seventh of the people in the Congo. Roman Catholic churches were even more numerous. Despite the turmoil and catastrophe in the Congo at the end of the colonial era, very few churches missed a single Sunday's service. In the absence of missionaries, national leadership more often bloomed than withered. There were even cases where medical assistants took over and performed operations in the absence of missionary medical doctors. But pastoral leadership of the churches was even far more indigenous.

Looking back in 1962, Latourette took note of the indigenous strength of the Christian movement in the non-Western world:

> The revolt among non-Europeans against imperialism and colonialism was accompanied by the deepened rootage of Christianity. Because Christianity had been associated with that imperialism and colonialism, the revolt might have been expected to lead to the waning of the Christian communities as alien enclaves. . . That was the case on the mainland of China. But elsewhere the result was the exact opposite. In land after land, the Christian churches grew and were increasingly self-governing, self-supporting, and self-propagating---as a long-cherished dream of Western missionaries had envisioned them.[4]

The Emergence of the National Church

As a matter of fact, some younger churches prospered greatly as the Western missionary apparatus withdrew during World War II. Not all the national leaders were immediately eager to take control of their own church movements, but generally they succumbed soon to the kind of freedom fever that raced through the non-Western world. In the few countries from which all missionaries had been deported during the war, many of the national leaders hotly resisted the re-establishment of any semblance of missionary domination when missionaries returned. Enormous confusion as well as vital dialogue resulted which continues to this day. Nationals began demanding what pained missionaries thought they had all along offered.

But generalizations are exceedingly hazardous. Complete independence had come to some younger churches long before World War II. Others were still dependent long after the war.

But as in the political realm so in the religious sphere foreign control tended to be modified or abrogated. Ready or not, self-determination was the "the thing." It was the fad or fashion. Some mission boards adopted sweeping policies which they tried to implement on every field, no matter what the relative maturity of the national church or the opinions of the field missionaries. Such boards often saw the picture more clearly than the field missionaries. There were two reasons for this: 1) missionaries intimately involved in a church tended to underestimate the maturity of the church, and 2) nationals on their part tended to overestimate the maturity of the church; they did this even if merely because they got cues from other missions and other parts of the world where immediate nationalization was stridently demanded. Just as in a family, there always seems to be disagreement between children and parents on the matter of the relative maturity of the younger generation---the parents generally underestimating and the children generally overestimating the possibilities. Thus the more sophisticated leaders in the younger churches often decried missionary imperialism despite the genuine, long-standing intentions of mission leaders to develop an indigenous church. The subject of the fate of the missions themselves is reserved for a separate section, but here we must note that there was a crescendo of interest in the question of when a church can be called indigenous.

The Indigenous Church

The very phrase <u>younger church</u> is part of the problem in the discussion of the indigenous church overseas. It may be better than <u>daughter church</u>, but a church is a community and therefore corresponds much more to a whole society than to an individual. True, it is possible to speak of older and younger <u>societies</u>. But many churches that have been <u>started</u> fairly recently by Western missionary endeavors are not <u>young</u> societies, but rather old societies with a new faith. Individuals in such Christian communities may at first be ignorant of the intricacies of foreign churchly patterns and practices, but insights from anthropology help us to see that such elements are only cultural. Western Christians on their part will appear just as ignorant about the cultural skills and structures of non-Western societies. Early Jesuits who compared the Indian languages of Mexico to Latin and complained of their deficiencies must have seemed to Indians almost hopelessly inept as they attempted to speak those languages, failing as they did to understand the marvelously complex grammatical and semantic structures behind them which even the Indian children understood. The same is true of those structural features of an indigenous society that may be intertwined in the ecclesiastical organization of an emergent church. The missionary who is determined to do things the way they are done in his homeland may in ignorance stress elements of his own indigenous cultural and linguistic patterns and in the long run end up witnessing a schism in which many will eventually withdraw from the mission church to form a church that better expresses their own long-standing cultural inheritance. The break-away church may thus be a new church in one sense, but this does not mean it can be properly or fully described by the term young since the new church will often incorporate aspects of an indigenous social structure far older than the imported church structure. Furthermore, the result may thereby achieve a stability and maturity of procedure which does not allow the comparison of that church to a new born baby unable to survive without tender loving care at every moment. Indeed, some have doubted that a mission-planted church ever needs to go through the transition of growing up into maturity and autonomy. Thus the larger question is not what is a younger church, but what is an indigenous church.

A. R. Tippett has shown that a church may be born indigenous, and that it is not age that produces indigeneity.[5] Donald McGavran suggests that "people movements" are more likely to produce Christian (but non-Western) styles of Christianity than are those movements which grow with painful slowness by converting individuals in the American style "one by one against the social tide."[6] Fortunately, mission agencies by 1970 conformed almost without exception to the belief that the new churches established in non-Western lands must be New Testament rather than Western. Yet in many cases this realization had become significant only during the period of the Retreat of the West. By that time

many longstanding Christian movements stemming from
nineteenth century missionary work were well established
in patterns imported from the West; during the confusion of
the Retreat it was too late for the leaders in those movements
to start over. Kenneth Cragg's recent book, Christianity in
World Perspective, talks about "nineteenth century mission
in twentieth century perspective." Reflecting on the younger
church situation,[7] he speaks of
the marked dominance of western cultural forms and
assumptions in the whole context of Christian thought,
worship, custom and practice among the nations of the
Gospel's dispersion. The geographical universality of
the Church, or nearly so, had been achieved only in the
context of a deep cultural partiality... For all its inclusive
impulse it is seen by most of the world as the perquisite
of western proprietors. Their near monopoly in its
expression and theology, their weight of numbers and
tradition, compromise its true dimensions in humanity
... It has often seemed, in its coming, an intruder and an
alien, a presence disruptive of existing societies and
ancestral cults, a trespasser among historic faiths and
the communities they have begotten... Men in their cultures have rallied in the reassertion of themselves or
hesitated, in wistful or dubious uncertainty, to know
whether the Christian promise of the human unity in
Christ would, or could, surmount the paradox of its
highly partial custody in modern history.

Fortunately such churches with their cultural overhang,
as McGavran puts it, were by no means the only kind of
younger churches prominent in the 1944-69 period. Some
churches, like the Mar Thoma Church of India and the Coptic
Church of Ethiopia, could not be called younger even in the
limited sense in which we have allowed that term. Though
such churches were not numerous, the category must be
mentioned.

A far larger group of churches, equally outside the
mission-planted stereotype, are the so-called independent
movements that began to gain greater notice in this period.
Some of them owed little or nothing of their development
to direct contributions from Western agencies. Others resulted as indigenizing splits from mission churches. David

Barrett, English editor of the World Christian Handbook for
1971, tabulated six thousand such indigenous movements in
Africa alone.[8] Bengt Sundkler, the first to highlight the evidences of such movements in his book Bantu Prophets, had
much earlier asserted that there were two thousand such
movements in South Africa alone.[9] Many were small and
confined to a single ethnic group. But some were very large
and spread to more than one country. One of these, the
Kimbangist Church of some one million adherents, joined
the World Council of Churches in 1969. By 1970, the two
fastest growing churches in Taiwan were of this type.[10] In
seeing the rapid growth and influence of such indigenous
Christian movements, some mission strategists have proposed that such churches might well be the church of the
future, and that in countries where they do not exist, perhaps
their emergence should be encouraged. It was well known
that the great bulk of Christian vitality in the United States
was the result of offshoot movements, whether Methodist,
the multitude of Baptist associations, or the increasingly
respected Pentecostal bodies. The latter group, though fast
growing, was not dominant in the United States during the
period under discussion, but by 1970 it outnumbered all
other Protestant bodies two to one in Latin America, and the
gap was still widening. One reason for the strength of the
Pentecostal churches of Brazil, for example, was that they
took seriously the indigenous animistic and spiritistic beliefs
of the people,[11] while Catholics and the older Protestant
churches tended to assume that such beliefs would disappear
if ignored.

Thus the indigenous church came to the fore. The prophet
Roland Allen [12] came into his own. It began to be seen that,
while a mission operation was often used of God to start
mighty movements to Christ, only indigenous churches,
which were native to the culture and recognized by their
members as their own, ever grew greatly. Indigenous
churches were favored by people movements, and people
movements which normally multiplied indigenous congregations were seen in many lands from Korea through Indonesia and Africa to Brazil, Chile, and Mexico. Through them
peoples of many levels of culture (primitives of New Guinea
and the cultured of Korea) and of many religions (Hindus,

Moslems, Animists, and Christopagans) entered the church. It began to be seen that the most significant movements would continue to occur through indigenous rather than indigenized churches, and probably by people movement routes. Viewed by mission strategists in 1970, the over-arching fact in the period of the Retreat of the West was not so much the Retreat itself but the continuous and mounting power of the non-Western Christian movement. Independent or not, mission-related or not, heretical or not, all kinds of Christianity in almost every situation displayed vigor and put down national roots in a way that could hardly have been believed in 1944. The younger churches were clearly not going to shrink and die away. Their existence, in the overwhelming majority of the cases, was no longer based on any significant foreign financial or organizational support, much less control.

The Evidences of a Major Movement

During most of the period, however, many Western Christians had little idea of the scope of the Christian movement in the non-Western countries. Many American Christians, for example, consistently tended to underestimate the growth of the younger churches for the simple reason that their knowledge extended only to the work of their particular denominations. During this period there was no popular magazine in English devoted exclusively to the overall progress of Christianity worldwide until the appearance of <u>World Vision Magazine</u> [13] in 1965. The collection of nickels and dimes in Sunday School offerings made missions appear to be a shoestring operation. Yet when all those nickels and dimes became integrated into the budgets of the overseas agencies, they were able to accomplish completely disproportionate results. As far back in history as 1910 there were already 180,000[14] students in secondary and college-level, Christian-mission institutions around the world. The leaders of the new nations were very often from this group. Virtually every representative of an African nation in the United Nations was a product of mission schools. Even while Nkrumah was in power in Ghana and leaned toward Russia, 90 percent of the schools in his country were run by foreign mission agencies or national Christian churches. The news media in the sixties gave excellent coverage to the heroic efforts of Tom Dooley, a Catholic doctor working independently in Laos, but eight hundred other American medical doctors working under Christian mission agencies went mainly unnoticed. When one was tragically murdered by guerilla forces in the Congo, many people assumed that he and perhaps Albert Schweitzer were the only missionary doctors in Africa. Commercial tourist agencies showered their customers with orientation, but rarely, if ever, pointed out that the largest experimental agricultural and medical centers in South Asia were Christian mission operations. Few tourists in Korea realized that medical missionaries over the years had produced over three thousand highly-trained medical doctors in Korea alone. How many knew that the largest engineering school in Latin America was a mission-sponsored university? Few people traveling in Indonesia realized that there were more Christians of the Presbyterian or Reformed tradition there than in the United States. This astonishing fact-gap was underlined by Lesslie Newbigin:[15]

> World Christianity... is the result of the great missionary expansion of the last two centuries. That expansion, whatever one's attitude to Christianity may be, is one of the most remarkable facts of human history. One of the oddities of current affairs, perhaps an understandable oddity under the circumstances, is the way in which the event is so constantly ignored or undervalued. It struck me as odd, for instance, in reading the voluminous report of a recent UNESCO conference on education in Africa, to find that, whereas something over 85 percent of all the school children in Africa are in Christian schools, the report did not, so far as I was able to detect, give even a hint that such a phenomenon as a Christian school exists.

In 1969 David Barrett, writing in the Church Growth Bulletin[16] projected that by the year two thousand Christianity would constitute 46 percent of the population of Africa.[17] Barrett's estimate was noted by Theodore L. Tucker of the African Department of the National Council of Churches in the United States. Time quoted him as saying that "for sheer size and rapidity of growth, this must be one of the most spectacular stories in history."[18] Yet hardly less spectacular has been the growth of various unrelated movements in different parts of Indonesia, only in part traceable to political factors following upon the massacre of communists in 1965. The sheer physical scope of the younger churches will be further discussed in the next section since it was during the same twenty-five-year period of their explosive expansion that the mounting power of the younger churches became decisively linked to the fate of worldwide Christianity.

The Younger Churches and the Ecumenical Movement

There is an ecumenical as well as a quantitative dimension to the growth of the younger churches. We have noted that the Kimbangist church became a member of the World Council of Churches. A relatively smaller Pentecostal church in Brazil joined at the same time. Earlier two Pentecostal churches in Chile had joined the World Council of Churches for a time. However the potential impact of the membership of the younger churches in the World Council remained to be seen, but could easily be imagined. When twenty-five new nations of Africa joined the United Nations between 1958 and 1963, the balance of power in that body decisively moved into the hands of non-Western nations who, by and large, took a "neutral" position in the Communist-capitalist polarization internal to the West. Would the same thing happen in the World Council of Churches? Who could tell? The situations were not quite parallel, since the major polarization in Western Christendom was not represented within the World Council in the way that the major polarization between Communist-capitalist nations was represented in the United Nations. Thus it was possible for new nations to join the U.N. without taking sides in the major political tension within the Western world. But a younger church joining the WCC would, by that very act, express her preference in regard to one of the major tensions within the Western Christian movement which resulted from the profound doubts of many concerning the legitimacy of the very existence of a structure like the World Council of Churches. This polarization in Western Christendom was particularly acute in the United States where the Roman Catholics and at least half of the

Protestants, including those whose churches were most rapidly growing, chose not to align themselves with the WCC. The significance of this tension in the United States could be seen in its reflection in the non-Western churches related to American mission agencies. In Asia, where mission personnel not aligned to the WCC were in the minority, the regional ecumenical council (the East Asia Christian Council) was very strong. In Africa, where the strongest missions were those supported by non-aligned churches, the ecumenical council (the All-Africa Council of Churches) had to compete with the Association of Evangelical Churches of Africa and Madagascar (AAEM). In Latin America the great dominance of missionaries represented non-aligned churches, and thus, as late as 1969, there was still no regional ecumenical council of churches, but only an organization working toward its establishment. On the other hand, there were dozens of interdenominational evangelical organizations performing all kinds of functions cooperatively in Latin America (e.g., publication, radio, theological education, air transportation, etc.). Some of these organizations embraced a very wide gamut of theological positions. The two mutually understandable languages — Spanish and Portuguese — tended to unite the majority of the people, but were not, in themselves, the only explanation for the cooperative spirit in Latin America.

The most significant feature of Christianity in Latin America during this period was the powerful emergence of Pentecostal churches, to the degree that by 1967 Pentecostals constituted 63 percent of all Protestants, their greatest strength being in Chile and Brazil.[19] With age and mounting strength, the Pentecostal churches became increasingly acceptable to the non-Pentecostal evangelicals and the non-evangelical Protestant communions. At the November, 1969 Congress on Evangelism in Bogota, a significant percentage of the delegates and the dominant majority of the local audience were Pentecostals. Their role in cooperative movements could not readily be predicted by early 1970, although two gatherings of Latin American Pentecostals in late 1969 went on record in an anti-ecumenical stance. Progressives in Catholic, historical Protestant, and Conservative Evangelical groups each hoped that the Pentecostal movement would eventually align itself with them. But it was not at all certain that alignment in cooperative and ecumenical bodies would be the same for any two Pentecostal churches, although their tendency to move in the same direction was enhanced by several evidences of increasing pan-Pentecostal unity, such as the emergence among Pentecostal laymen of a worldwide "Full Gospel Businessmen's Association."

It was a curious fact that while in the United States five (and later eight) older denominations strove valiantly to merge through the Consultation on Church Union (COCU), probably a new denomination a day was springing up with vigorous life in the non-Western world. The cause of organic unity, at least when considered worldwide, seemed clearly outrun by abounding diversity in the so-called younger churches.

The Theological Problem of Diversity

Granted the reassuring fact that the so-called younger churches were now a great movement, unbelievably rooted, durable, and nationally supported, how were Christians to view their irreconcilable diversity in form, theology, ecclesiology, and even ethics? Would not their very diversity drive Westerners to rethink their traditional perspectives about the internal development and structure of their churches? In the historical background of the Western Christian, different "confessions" had emerged from the different language and culture areas of Europe. When those confessions collided in the United States, they became somewhat modified from their related churches back in Europe, but they basically survived and became large denominations. The chief reason for their workability in the New World was the fact that their membership was made up of people who were already culturally attuned to church traditions from the Old World. It was to be expected that European distinctives would similarly be transplanted in the churches of South Africa, Australia, Argentina, or any other land where the population was made up primarily of people of European background. But it was quite a different thing for churches being founded in areas of vast non-Western populations to be expected to adopt a European Christian tradition in the same way. In those few cases where this for a time seemed to have happened, the new church may eventually, like a heart transplant, be rejected by an immunization reaction. Thus, with the drastic lessening of missionary domination during the Retreat of the West, there developed to an extent never before anticipated the true kaleidoscope of potential diversity in the Christian movement.

But in the face of this burgeoning diversity, the serious question became urgent: are these new plants flowers or weeds? This question was tough and profound. It was raised insistently during the Retreat of the West more than at any other time since Paul insisted on the legitimacy of a Christianity that was culturally non-Jewish. In Paul's time, Jews and even some Jewish Christians, doubted the validity of the Greek formulation. As late as 1968 that issue was still very much alive, when a Jewish rabbi[20] with magnificent logic maintained that Christianity was merely the result of the essence of the Jewish faith being damaged and paganized through contact with the Greek culture. In parallel fashion, Roman Christians at the time of the Reformation insisted that the Lutheran formulation was invalid because it was the result of the German culture damaging true (i.e., Roman) Christianity, while many Lutherans felt the Roman formulation was pagan. Latourette did not take sides. He merely commented that the Roman Catholic church

> is in reality the church of Latin Europe, a continuation in a religious form of the Roman Empire, and it has had and continues to have its main strength in Southwestern Europe, the portion of the world that was most permeated by the culture and speech of Rome.[21]

The same issue was the basis of the famous century-long (1643-1742) Chinese Rites Controversy, in which the Jesuits insisted upon the preservation of certain Chinese cultural forms. The Papal Bull of 1742 which reversed their emphasis incurred the wrath of the Chinese emperor, introduced deep confusion into the ranks of the mission force, and brought a halt to the physical advance of Christianity in China.[22] Protestants generally have strongly opposed Roman traditions specifically, yet have maintained their own European customs, even in non-Western lands. Hesitance and confusion about the legitimacy or illegitimacy of cultural overlays in Christianity lay behind the resistance of Lutheran mission leaders in India to the idea of separate congregations of the same denomination being established in two sharply distinct sections of Indian villages---one among the depressed classes and another among the middle classes. Meanwhile other modern Lutherans in their turn ignored (while some championed as functionally "Lutheran") the fast-growing indigenous Chinese churches of Taiwan mentioned previously.[23]

A wide variety of opinions, strongly held, marked the discussion of this issue. As a reaction to the persistent tendency on almost everyone's part to define true Christianity simply in terms of the church of his own specific cultural tradition, some thinkers went to the opposite extreme of postulating all traditions as equal and even including the non-Christian religions as functional equivalents to Christianity. Some did not go quite so far, but regarded non-Christian religions as adequately improvable through contact and dialogue with Christians. In the attempt to universalize the Christian faith a famous Catholic theologian, Leslie Dewart,[24] advocated so sweeping a de-Hellenization of the Roman tradition that one of his books was suppressed. Nevertheless the de-Westernization of Christianity was widely assumed to be necessary, and even the conservative evangelical theologian, Carl F. Henry,[25] ventured reflections on a _logos_ of revelation to be found in all religions. Some indeed continued to equate, say, Reformed theology with "the whole counsel of God." Yet when plans for a new China Graduate School of Theology were being discussed late in 1969, it was the consensus of the American advisory board that this school should not settle on Lutheran, Arminian, or Reformed theology, but should consider as almost its primary task that of the development of a truly indigenous Chinese theological expression of the Christian faith. This same view had long been the conviction of Japanese scholars.[26] In Africa, for example, a missionary anthropologist, Donald R. Jacobs,[27] attempted a preliminary manual of theology that was designed to speak meaningfully within the world view of African animist peoples. Latin American leaders cried out for a distinctive Latin American theology. And the phrase "Black Theology" began to be heard in the United States. The ever increasing diver-

sity in the theological spectrum of Christianity as it mani-
fested itself in these varied movements might have dismayed
even the most hardy optimists in the ecumenical tradition
represented by the World Council of Churches. The com-
paratively few differences in theology resulting from the
cultural decentralization inherent in the Reformation could
only remotely be compared to the theological diversity
emerging in the aftermath of the Retreat of the West. Amidst
all this diversity, the definition of the "core" of Christianity
to which Latourette referred in 1955[28] became both increasingly urgent and complicated.

According to one observer,[29] one common denominator
amid the diversity of the independent Christian movements
in Africa was the relationship of their emergence to the
availability of a translation of the Bible in the vernacular
of the group involved. He said that with a vernacular Bible
in their hands, the independent leadership in many cases
wanted no further help from the white man, except perhaps
from foreign Christians, not representing foreign mission
agencies or churches, who would come merely to teach them
how to read the Bible in its original languages. They would
thus be able ultimately to verify and do over the white man's
translation upon which they must depend in the interim.
Down through history, the Bible in the vernacular has produced two results: 1) It has, on the one hand, enabled a
retranslation and reinterpretation more understandable in
each particular indigenous cultural milleu, and yet 2) it has
also tended eventually to lessen the differences between
Christians, weeding out all sorts of quasi-Christian ideas.
Thus despite differences which to Western Christians appear
great, the diverse denominations of the West, as seen against
a background of Hinduism, Confucianism, Islam, or animism
often appear remarkably alike. The Bible when accepted as
the Word of God and the rule of faith and practice inevitably
allows all kinds of cultural diversity, yet holds this diversity
under certain bonds and gradually brings more and more
functional unity between diverse forms of Christianity.

One specialized mission agency, the Wycliffe Bible Translators, by 1970 had 2114 members, many of whom were ex-
pert linguists dedicated to the task of producing vernacular
translations of the Bible for all the peoples of the earth.

Its strength reflected the widespread consensus that the Bible would somehow be necessary for a truly indigenous church of any kind.

There remained, however, the seemingly impenetrable mystery surrounding the ultimate purpose of God for the disparate peoples of mankind. If unity neither required nor suggested outward uniformity as a goal---and this seemed a near consensus---it nevertheless seemed true that no one part of the body could say to the other "I have no need of you." A monolithic uniformity in an age of unprecedented diversity began to appear as unthinkable as total independence. It was in this sense that R. Pierce Beaver spoke of "unity in the midst of diversity in the household of faith." [30]

In any case, it became increasingly clear that Christian vitality did not have its sole source in the West: the changing balance of political power was accompanied by a shifting of the center of Christianity. At the very least it could be said that the West no longer had a monopoly on Christianity. In Beaver's words again, "a geographical 'Christendom' in the West (had) been replaced by a 'diffused Christendom' composed of churches and disciples all around the world."[31] Thus the fate of the younger churches became decisively involved in that of Christianity itself.

3

THE FATE OF
CHRISTIANITY

One of the most thrilling statements characterizing the period of the Retreat of the West was made a few months before it began. In 1942 Archbishop William Temple spoke of "the great new fact of our era" as "a Christian fellowship which now extends into almost every nation."[32] Long in the making, this "great new fact" had already begun to be a reality prior to the beginning of the Retreat, but then when the tide seemed to be flowing against the West on every side during the twenty-five-year Retreat, the great new fact became immensely substantiated as the emerging overseas churches stood firm and constituted a bulwark against undue Western pessimism resulting from the apparent reverses of the period. Latourette's lectures at the Rice Institute in 1948 referred to this great new fact in an elaborated form which became a whole book, The Emergence of a World Christian Community. In the final chapter of the fifth volume of Christianity in a Revolutionary Age he noted the phenomenon succinctly in five statements about Christianity "in the world outside Europe."[33]

(1) Christianity was continuing to spread and was more widely represented than it or any other religion had ever been.

(2) By 1962 that spread was achieved less through government support and direction than at any time since the conversion of Constantine early in the fourth century.

(3) Christianity was becoming more deeply rooted among more peoples than at any previous time.

(4) Christianity was having a wider effect on mankind outside Europe than it or any other religion had
ever exerted.

(5) Christians were coming together in a global
fellowship embracing both Europeans and non-Europeans
as they had not previously done.

Variations of this list appeared in many of his writings
throughout the period.

Communism and Christianity

In spite of the strength of Christianity, most people had
the impression that the religion sweeping the world was
Communism. As a religion Communism was not much
more than a passion for running governments in a certain
way. It propagated the conviction that all other benefits
would flow from the proper design of government, even the
creation of a new humanity, a new man. For a while following
World War II, especially after the Communists gained control
of China, it did seem that the whole world might go that way.
A brief alliance between the Russian and Chinese governments, the election results in Kerala, India, the growing
Communist power in Indonesia, all engendered widespread
fear that Communism would take over the whole non-Western
world and perhaps the Western world as well. Castro's
Cuba brought this possibility home to the United States,
and produced a deep-seated reaction on the part of millions
of Americans who had never before become personally concerned about Communism as a force in world affairs. The
near-fatal impact of Communism on the churches of China,
North Korea, and North Vietnam dimmed the prospects for
Christianity in the non-Western world even further. Some
formerly enthusiastic supporters of missionary work transferred their interest and funds to anti-Communist organizations and conservative political groups.

These clouds of fear diminished as the Russian-Chinese
axis splintered, the Communists were brutally expelled from
Indonesia, and the export of Castro-Communism to the rest
of Latin America was checked by rightist reactions. (Some
observers wondered if Castro may not have "vaccinated"
Latin America against Communism.) The forceful occupation

of Hungary and Czechoslovakia by the Russians further tar-
nished the Communist image. Rising tensions of various
kinds within the Communist sphere also dimmed the hopes
of this anti-religious religion. By 1970 it seemed increasingly impossible for Russia and China to fulfill whatever
plans they may have had for a new colonialism in the recently
independent countries of the non-Western world. Apparently
Russian and Chinese imperialism had appeared too late in
history, in a kind of anti-climactic colonialism born out of
due time. The great watershed was 1945.

Communism also failed to compete with Christianity on
purely religious grounds. Christianity faced serious difficulties under anti-religious Communist regimes, but Communism proved to be less than competitive as a religion. It
was able to topple governments, and to oppress Christianity
for secular reasons, but it could not readily win the faith of
the masses, especially traditional rural people, or people
without a prior, Westernized sense of material values. Even
Polish university students complained that it did not offer
answers to the ultimate questions of life, such as the origin
of matter or man's ultimate destiny. Even in countries controlled by Communism, the Communist parties constituted
a very small percentage of the people. Communist cells
infiltrated cities and student movements across the world,
but actually were vastly outnumbered by cells of Christian
fellowship that penetrated a much wider spectrum of the
layers of society, both rural and urban and, in the long run,
proved more durable and tenacious than the Communist
variety. And why not? Communist cells had borrowed from
the Wesleyan "class meeting" the idea of confession, but not
that of forgiveness; they demanded good deeds, but did not
insist on love. Marx, Lenin, Stalin, Mao, Castro---not one
of these men could be compared to Jesus Christ except,
perhaps, in up-dated promises of social justice, but even
such promises were not readily fulfilled.

If Communism was not therefore the menace to overseas
Christianity that some had thought it would be, what about
its impact on the heartlands of Western Christianity?
Latourette devoted thirty-eight pages to "Christianity in
Revolutionary Russia" in Volume Four of Christianity in a
Revolutionary Age, and his comments are surprising. He

steadfastly maintained that

> so far as statistics could be obtained...in proportion to
> the population of Christian ancestry, attendance at church
> services in 1961 was higher in Russia than in Sweden or
> Denmark and in parts of France, especially in the cities,
> and may even have been higher than among the Protes-
> tant elements in England. It was certainly higher in
> Moscow than in Copenhagen, Stockholm, Hamburg,
> Berlin, and Paris. In Western Europe most of the forces
> working against Christianity were not as outspokenly
> opposed to the faith as in Russia...But...corrosive
> currents associated with the revolutionary age were
> almost if not quite as potent as in Russia. Here is a
> thought-provoking parallel for the appraisal of the
> effect of the revolutionary age on Christianity and of
> the vitality of the faith.[34]

For some it was staggering to realize that in Russia after
half a century of Communism Christianity was faring little
worse than it was in Western Europe. This was obviously
no cause for rejoicing. The basic problem appeared to be
secularism in both Eastern and Western Europe rather than
Communism itself. It made some wonder whether gains in
the overseas churches could be viewed optimistically if in
the homeland Christianity was tried and found wanting.

Consequently, in *Christianity in a Revolutionary Age*
Latourette's extensive section on Christianity in the United
States was a picture of only qualified optimism. He noted
both positive and negative features, and called it a "complex
multiform record." He could not quite bring himself to
acknowledge the decline of the Student Volunteer Movement,
and mercifully did not live to see its final official demise in
the spring of 1969. On the other hand, neither did he refer
to the rising interdenominational influence for missionary
recruitment of the Inter-Varsity Missionary Conventions.
But no one has so faithfully described in so great detail the
continuing, increasing complexity and vitality of the Christian movement, even in the Western world. He decried all
thought of a "Post-Christian" world as "glib...naive and
hasty." [35]

The Impression of a Dwindling Movement

An objective approach to any movement is an examination of its physical dimension. It is generally hazardous to assume that an existing rate of growth will be maintained in the future, and one would not be wise to predict either inevitable success or failure by this method. Yet if predictions are to be made, the arithmetic should be accurate. However, during this twenty-five-year period there was a great deal of erroneous arithmetic, and in consequence much confusion and misinformation. Many took it for granted that Christianity was dying out and could only struggle on trying to withstand the onslaughts of resurgent non-Christian religions as long as possible. For example, in 1969 Kenneth Cragg said,

In so far as religions have their relative importance determined by numbers, Christianity is rapidly losing ground... In very few Asian and African societies does population increase allow the Christian communities anything but a sharply declining percentage. If the objective of the Christian presence in the world is to possess all nations in their masses, it is manifestly succeeding less and less.[36]

If such a highly respected scholar could speak in such erroneous terms, others who haven't even attempted to employ the fairly complicated calculations of quantitative growth rates can surely be excused for voicing the same sentiments. Thanks to the existence among missionaries of a number of former engineers, these comments did not go unchallenged. Early in 1970, it was pointed out[37] that the fact that the number of Christians in the Western world seemed to be dwindling was in part due to the use of a more stringent definition of the term Christian, and that the idea that Christianity was dwindling in the non-Western countries was, for the most part, simply bad arithmetic. One important point, if one is going to make predictions as does Cragg, is to realize that rates of growth are more important than increases in absolute numbers, during a given period. The most detailed calculations for a particular area are those for Africa done by David Barrett.[38] His figures show that the net increase in the number of

Christians has at no time ever been equal to the number of additional non-Christians in that continent, but even so, for the continent as a whole, he projects that the relatively faster rates of growth of the various sectors of Christianity (Protestant, Roman Catholic, African Independent) will not only establish Christianity as the major religion of Africa by the year 2000 but will see it winning a steadily larger proportion of the total population (3% in 1900, 28% in 1970, 46% in 2000).

The most glaring quantitative fallacy in the pessimistic thinking of the time was the assumption that the population explosion would inevitably force a decline in the proportions of Christianity. Yet the biological growth of a human population is relatively slow (a world average of 1.9 percent in 1969), and is by nature outclassed by the potential growth of Christianity, or any other faith which not only grows biologically but wins adherents by conversion, since an additional mechanism is involved. In 1964 R. Pierce Beaver cited statistics to show that Protestantism had increased eighteen-fold in sixty years in the non-Western world.[39] Yet the population increase was only two-fold. Christian growth in other non-Western continents has not everywhere reached the dramatic proportions seen in Africa. But in almost every place the Christian community was growing as fast or faster than the population—not in absolute numbers per year, but in growth rate and therefore in percentage of the population.

By 1970 some countries such as Brazil, saw an annual growth for Protestants of 11.3 percent,[40] which means doubling in seven years (while the general population will take twenty-four to double). This, of course, is no longer growth within a non-Western culture. Although the new Brazilian Protestants mainly come from elements of the population which are "least Catholic,"[41] it would be unrealistic to count such people as being utterly untouched by the influence of Christianity. The Pentecostal churches, which are the major element in the rapid growth cited, draw members from animistic religions as well as from a nominal Catholic faith, but even so this is not a phenomenon comparable to the advancing front of Christianity in an Africa whose population does not primarily derive from even a semi-Christianized Europe.

Pentecostal growth in Brazil thus compares more nearly to the growth of a church in Western Europe, North America, Australia, or New Zealand. All such growth partakes to some extent of renewal rather than the conversion of peoples previously untouched by Christianity. Evangelistically minded U.S. churches, well acquainted with the process of "winning people to Christ" in this renewal sense in North America at times do not understand what is involved in evangelizing a totally non-Western people. For example, in early 1970 one could generalize, with admitted oversimplification, that in the Western part of the Western world there were four major varieties of Christians: 1) Pentecostals, who considered themselves also Evangelicals, 2) Evangelicals,[42] who considered themselves also Protestants, 3) Protestants, who were increasingly able to admit that they were basically Catholic, and 4) Roman Catholics. Each of these movements tended to consider its parent movement(s) cold and formal or lifelessly institutional. Each of the first three considered itself a life-giving renewal with respect to its immediate parent. But insofar as one group was renewed by the emergence of the other within its ranks, the type of church growth involved— however vital and worthwhile it might have been—was not strictly comparable to the kind of Christian growth we have been concerned about in the non-Western countries.

The mere fact, however, that Western Christendom was engaged in this type of internal ferment shows that the era under consideration was by no means post-Christian. Christianity was not dwindling, but a changing, seething, forward movement in both the Western and non-Western worlds.

Christianity in a World Demanding Change

By 1970 in the Western world, Christianity despite its cultural momentum seemed to be facing immense opposition to its institutional structure. Isolated examples of angry young men in the fifties, and a much more massive revolt of the youth in the sixties involved not only the rejection of traditional forms of Christianity but also the traditional forms of everything else. Small groups of beatniks evolved into the relatively widespread phenomenon of the hippie movement. A large factor in the unrest was the apparent hopelessness of military and political power as it might be exerted by the West in trouble spots of the non-Western world. The period of the Retreat of the West was disappointing to Westerners not merely because of the withdrawal of the colonial apparatus. Deep dismay about the very hopes of mankind had resulted from one of the stinging lessons of the Second World War: man was incorrigibly warlike. Even civilized Western man found himself involved at Auschwitz in a genocide unbelievably inhuman, yet perhaps all too human. In Reinhold Niebuhr's writings a new, brutally honest form of theology arose which revived the belief in original sin and tended rather to underestimate man's potential. Philosphical acids of every kind corroded and ate away Christian faith, especially in university circles. Existentialism of several varieties came into vogue. But whether it was that of Kierkegaard, Sartre, Bonhoeffer, or Hoekendijk, existentialism always tended to give in to a pessimism about the plans, the institutions, and the material hopes of both man and the church.

This pessimism had a profound effect upon the Christian church as a whole. It crushed the idealistic hopes of some. For others it demanded a return to a more orthodox faith with the hope that somehow orthodoxy could return to society the stability it had lost. Neo-orthodoxy, for example, blasting as it did the rosy hopes of an earlier liberalism, became a widely accepted theological stance found in one degree or another in most seminaries, whether of the more conservative or the more liberal bent.

One widespread reaction was a rejection of all organized religion as such, yet at the same time a grasping after a simple faith not easily found in the churches. In this period a few radical theologians spoke of "the death of God," but their choice of terms to define a redirection of faith was generally rejected so that even the momentary notoriety of their "death" theory tended to bring about a renewed interest in religion. The hippie movement sought a kind of religious faith in the love of nature and an emotion-releasing use of allegedly mind-expanding drugs. Many liberal Catholics

became involved in an underground Catholic church movement, led by Catholic laymen, radical priests, and at times
excommunicated married priests. Youth completely un-
acquainted with the churches felt that Jesus was their kind
of man, and formed simple creeds of their own, writing songs
about Jesus the revolutionary in the popular tunes and beat.
There was a seeking for emotional expression in religion,
in the increasing strength of the Pentecostal movement, in
the "charismatic" movement in the older Protestant
churches and in Catholic circles, and in experimentation
with emotion in various types of non-Christian religions.
"Sensitivity training" and small-group "honesty" became
important in many quarters, ranging from the business
sphere to the seminaries.   Stress was placed upon social
justice.   The private and public morality of public officials
came to be judged with such severity that high ranking
government officials were asked to resign because of nepotism, bribery, or the semi-illegal use of funds, acts that in
some cases might have escaped notice in an earlier era.
Yet organized crime was stronger in the United States than
it had ever been in history.

Perhaps one of the most striking instances of revolt
against tradition was what happened during these twenty-
five years in the Roman Catholic Church.   It was as if a
great dam which had held back a flood of water for centuries
suddenly was opened by Pope John XXIII and the Vatican II
ecumenical council which he called. All sorts of ideas and
innovations burst forth as a result.   There was a rejection
of a meaningless mass recited in a dead language, and for
the first time in centuries lay people knew and understood
the implications of what was said.   Catholic scholars and
priests alike returned to biblical studies, stressing daily
practical Christian holiness of life. The centrality of Mary
was called into question, as was the holiness of priestly
celibacy, and the episcopal authority of the Pope himself.
Priests and nuns gave up their sacred vows, at first singly,
then in groups ranging up to a hundred or more. Clerical
garb and religious habits were adapted to twentieth-century
dress.   Liberal Catholic scholars insisted that the church
should not be an institution, but a movement, and they sometimes left the institution in order better to serve Christ in

His movement. [43]

The massive revolt against tradition did not seem to be aimed specifically at Christianity, although the church was certainly adjudged part of the establishment. Some took heart in the relative absence of specific criticism of Christ and Christian faith, and sought to discern the meaning of a Christian faith apart from the institutional structure of the church. Van Leeuwen [44] seemed to say that Christianity, both beyond and apart from its institutional expression, can be and actually is a secular faith that is cutting away the very roots of all the non-Christian religions, perhaps even its own institutional roots!

Thus in the sixties some of the traditional Protestant churches expressed the feeling that the organized church could not be a goal in itself, but that the target must be the world: "God so loved the world." The 1968 meeting of the World Council of Churches in Uppsala, Sweden emphasized that the "world's agenda" must guide the strategy of the church, and that the structures of society—not merely the faith of individuals in society—had to be Christianized. Moderates on both sides of this issue acknowledged the values in the opposite positions. The contest was in part the continuation of a long-standing tension between those cultural and theological distinctives (by no means merely a conservative-liberal dimension) that belong to the spiritual descendents of the Evangelical Awakening and those who felt closer to the older Protestantism. (A parallel tension could be seen in the Roman tradition.) One side could not distinguish between the other's "social conscience" and mere "humanism," while the other side could not distinguish between the first side's "Pietism" and "Quietism."

A far more serious difference of perspective existed in conflicting views about the proper organizational structure of the church. The Evangelical Awakening was born within an established Protestantism. Until Wesley's death the Methodist movement was, hopefully, a non-conflicting and renewing movement within the state church. It was, in the stream of classical Pietism, a "church-within-the-church" —a "believers' church" within a state church. Its members, for the most part, eventually withdrew to form a free church, but before that happened, its example went a long way toward establishing a Protestant parallel to the Catholic order, the idea of an elite, committed society within a church. This same kind of structure was shortly to be harnessed for the purpose of sending out missionaries. All of the early Protestant missionary societies that burst forth in profusion between 1792 and 1820 had this structure. Even boards that were not interdenominational (but unofficially supported within a single denomination) were, in their origin, elite societies unrelated to the on-going official budget structure of those denominations and their congregations.

By 1970 the vast majority of all denominational mission agencies had become tied to the overall administrative budgets of the respective denominations, and being thus tied were inevitably affected by anti-establishment and anti-institutional feelings on the part of the membership. Mission societies on the continent were still technically separate from the church structures, even though many, for theological reasons, felt this ought not to be. Nevertheless, a host of new agencies accelerated their growth during the period, primarily those that maintained financial autonomy from denominational budgets. These John A. Mackay compared [45] to Catholic orders. Their existence seemed to indicate a continuing eagerness on the part of Western Christians to give of their lives and their substance in a cause aimed primarily at the spiritual needs of man.

The whole matter of the specific mechanism of mission is the concern of the next section. Here we merely observe throughout this whole period the heightening of both interest and tension in the realm of the Christian faith and its proper expression. Traditional forms shuddered under the strain. The greatest specific pressures were brought to bear upon the Roman communion by the prevailing mood of decentralization and individual participation, and it looked as if even more monumental changes would take place in the Catholic church in the next few years. There was no real evidence of a net decrease in Christian faith, even in the Western homeland of Christianity. The future of Christianity was not in doubt, although its traditional Western dress was not likely to continue unchanged in the Western world, much less in the non-Western world.

4

THE FATE OF

THE MISSIONS

We began with a glance at the impact of twenty-five unbelievable years upon the non-Western lands. We saw the emergence of scores of new nations and the dismantling of the colonial offices of the Western governments. We inquired anxiously about the fate of the so-called younger churches apparently left behind by the withdrawal of the white man. We noted the impact of the period upon Christianity itself, even in its Western homeland.

We have now to look at the impact of this period upon the missions, the sending agencies—those specialized organizations that deliberately engaged in the recruitment of people and/or funds in order to propagate the faith across some kind of cultural barrier, usually in a foreign country. We will need to define them since they are in some ways a peculiar phenomenon. We will need to try to understand how they grew or declined, and how their purposes, perspectives, and support patterns changed. But first let us simply note some of the more obvious, outward ways in which these twenty-five years had an impact on the missions.

The Cutting of Roots

First of all, both the First and the Second World Wars directly and drastically affected mission work. When Germany lost her overseas colonies in the First World War, her missions were taken over and the work carried on by the mission agencies of enemy countries. World War I was thus a proving ground for Christian collaboration between missionaries and mission organizations who were political enemies. At the treaty of Versailles, J. H. Oldham of England achieved the nearly impossible by introducing a clause that prevented the confiscation of German mission properties. World War II was immensely unsettling. German, French, and English-based missions all over the world, vastly greater in scope now than in 1917, received more than six million dollars raised mainly in other countries to keep them operating. In their story of the Orphaned Missions written in 1949, Latourette and William Richie Hogg told how at one point Dutch missionaries in what is now Indonesia "assessed themselves a small amount each month to help the German missionaries among the Bataks."[46] Despite such heartwarming efforts on the part of many different kinds of people, unbelievable, heartbreaking difficulties ensued. When Hitler marched into Holland, German missionaries in Sumatra were interned by the Dutch government. Wives and families were left behind as the men were shipped to India, not to see them again for seven years. At the same time, the British authorities in India allowed German missionaries to continue their mission work. Fortunately, in Northern Sumatra, the Christians, already constituting 30 percent of the Bataks, were quite able to carry on and indeed to increase in number. In many other cases this was not so true.

The overall influence of the two world wars on the pattern of missions was inevitably to cut away European roots and to shift the base of missions more and more to the New World. By 1945 the center of gravity for Protestant mission support had already long been in North America. Although the center of gravity of Catholic missions remained in Europe despite the travail of the world wars, a great deal of new initiative and support developed on the Western side of the Atlantic due to the impact of the wars.

The Closing of Doors

A second major blow suffered by mission agencies during this period was the closing of several non-Western countries to missionary work. Unlike the temporary evacuation of missionaries from Japanese occupied territories in the Pacific during World War II, the missionary withdrawal from China was massive. To some it seemed permanent. This forced exodus dealt a telling blow to the hopes and aspirations of many mission agencies. Deep-seated hesitance about traditional mission goals produced an attitude that became curiously institutionalized by virtue of the fact that the returned "China hands" (former missionaries to China) came to occupy a disproportionately large number of the administrative jobs in those many mission agencies which had been heavily committed in China. A mentality developed which seemed to concentrate on every new indication that another government was likely to exclude missionaries (Burma, Ceylon, India, etc.), and it tended to regard agencies that forged ahead hopefully as being either ignorant or stubborn in view of the facts.

The largest single agency working in China---the China Inland Mission---was greatly reduced in size by the retreat of the Westerner from China. It extended its name by adding Overseas Missionary Fellowship and transferred hundreds of its workers into mission activities among Chinese and non-Chinese peoples on the rim of South East Asia, but nevertheless experienced for a time an overall decline in workers.

The Deepening Pessimism

At the International Missionary Council meeting at Tambaram in 1938 the impending chaos of World War II was clearly felt, but a bold summons was made to biblical faith and church-centered evangelism. The Whitby Conference in 1947 followed in the wake of the Second World War and its still hopeful notes were based upon new awareness of the reality of the younger churches, and for a partnership in obedience with them in pushing forward. But by 1952 at Willingen in the words of James Sherer, formerly in China:

The Western missionary movement was still reeling from the recent shock of the closing of its largest field, China. There was also a painful awareness that many institutional expressions of Christianity had lost their missionary impetus, and that the Church was too often on the defensive, conserving its resources rather than advancing into the world with the gospel. The world mission faced "other faiths of revolutionary power...in the full tide of victory." Its only recourse was to take its stance at the foot of the cross and to place its confidence in the ultimate triumph of Christ's "hidden kingdom." [47]

One of the most acute observers of the scene following the Second World War was Max Warren, General Secretary of the Church Missionary Society of the Anglican Church. His appraisal of the situation in 1953 was typical of the best thinking of many mission leaders.[48]

At Whitby, in 1947, we hoped that the most testing days of the Christian mission, at least for our generation, lay behind us...But here at Willingen clouds and thick darkness surround the (future) and we know with complete certainty that the most testing days of the Christian mission in our generation lie just ahead...We have to be ready to see the day of missions, as we have known them, as having already come to an end.

Looking back from 1970 it seemed as though Latourette's analysis in Missions Tomorrow written in 1936 would have been helpful:

More basic still as a factor in declining or stationary incomes and personnel of missions is an uncertainty as to the validity of the Christian faith. Nineteenth-century Protestant missions, we have seen, were in large part an expression of a series of religious awakenings unprecedented in the history of Protestantism. It was out of the burning conviction of Pietism, Evangelicalism, and and the revivals which punctuated the history of nineteenth-century Protestantism in the Anglo-Saxon world and the Continent of Europe that missionaries went out to the ends of the earth and that funds were contributed for their support. It was from the Moody movement, the latest of these great revivals, that the Student Volunteer Movement was born and that a large proportion of the leaders came who headed the missionary enterprise in the day just closing. In many quarters the fires of this enthusiasm are burning low...Great bodies of youth have drifted entirely away from the Church, or at best preserve only a nominal connection. To these the old slogans of Evangelicalism sound faint and hollow, like the dying echoes of a bygone age. In many circles in which Evangelical conviction was once strong an easy-going liberalism now prevails, with the kind of tolerance which is sprung of skepticism as to the validity of its own inherited beliefs. Many, even among the clergy, are seeking in a social revolution a substitute for the religious convictions for which their communions officially stand but to which they as individuals can no longer subscribe. From such a Christianity no vigorous foreign mission enterprise can be expected. Unless new revivals reinvigorate it, it is doomed, even in its own strongholds.

Fortunately for the foreign missionary enterprise and for Christianity, these somber shades are only part of the picture... Christian missions have ever been a minor-ity movement. Almost always the really active support of missions in a congregation has rested upon two or three convinced and devoted souls---to their glory be it said, usually women... Our reading of Christian history has accustomed us to see Him break forth in unexpected places where souls have opened themselves to Him and and been made great by the touch of His Spirit... The new movements which saved Protestantism and started it off on its great nineteenth-century career did not emerge from the intelligentsia who sought to defend the faith by logic-proof intellectual arguments. It is not that God shuns the well-known centers, for sometimes His great saints and prophets arise from them... We believe that He will break forth again, even though it may be in most unpredictable quarters. He, we are convinced, is the great factor of the age into which we are moving, as He was in the age out of which we have come... We believe that souls will be found to respond to God and that to-morrow as yesterday new movements will demonstrate His power.[49]   (Italicization added.)

The Unbelievable Record

If the mood did not change due to Latourette's advice in

1936, nor due to a later book looking back to it,[50] at least those words proved prophetic. New movements did appear: independent churches of every sort sprouted in the non-Western lands; new mission agencies sprang into existence "in most unpredictable quarters", undaunted by the apparent hopelessness of the situation. Figure Three shows that the number of missionaries under some agencies leveled off during this period, while still other organizations were able to grow significantly in the radically changing soil of the Retreat of the West. The latter cast fresh eyes on the non-Western populations and ferreted out many new and unprecedentedly responsive places for work among the two billion non-Christians of the world. They were able furthermore to interpret their needs to Christians in the West so as to recruit vast new resources of personnel and funds. Figure Four shows that the total Protestant missionary force of all lands, while suffering dips during each of the two world wars, steadily increased. Later figures trace this increase largely to the appearance and subsequent growth of the newer agencies.

Figure Five, taken by permission from a leading periodical, compares the growth of certain specific U. S. mission organizations during this period, and was perhaps designed to imply that mergers were hard on mission giving. Mergers were surely not the only factor causing decline in missionary support. It may have been that mergers tended to produce an increasingly conglomerate budget or increasing bigness and diversity within a sending church, and for this reason tended to reduce the interest and sense of responsibility of individual members toward organizational goals. However, the age of a denomination tends to produce diversity too, as it grows out into various regions of a country and into different strata and sectors of society. Smallness and newness tend to assure the unanimity that allows concerted action. It is significant that the churches on the left are older and the churches on the right are younger, and that on the extreme right the last four agencies do not represent churches at all, but appeal simply to mission-minded people within the churches, whether new or old.

An excellent analysis of the overall picture of North American Protestant missions in regard to the statistical

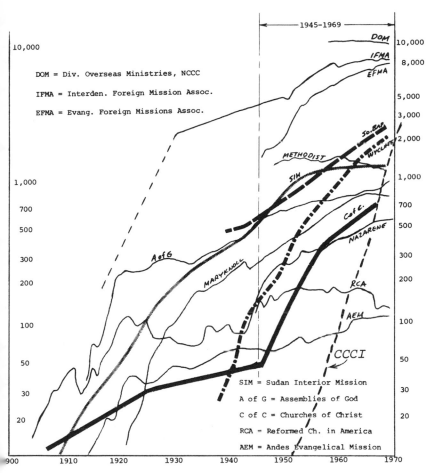

Figure 3:   GROWTH IN PERSONNEL OVERSEAS OF SELECTED MISSION AGENCIES

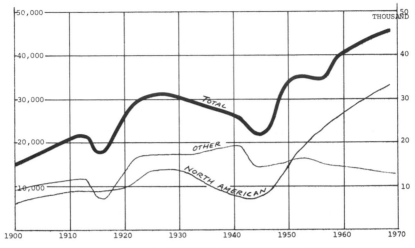

Figure 4: PROTESTANT FOREIGN MISSIONARY PERSONNEL

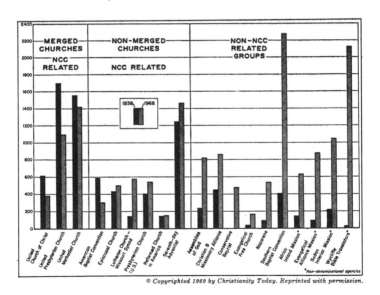

Figure 5: COMPARATIVE STATISTICS OF OVERSEAS MISSIONARY FORCES

growth of different kinds of mission agencies, the new psychological barriers to recruitment, and the survival of mission personnel for the period 1960-68 is a brief article entitled "Changing Patterns of Missionary Service in Today's World" by David M. Stowe.[51] Figure Six is drawn from data he gives and again shows the percentage increase in income to be significantly greater for the newer churches or non-denominational agencies, most of which are not part of the National Council of Churches.

Not only was there growth on the part of specific agencies, there were many new agencies, and even new associations of agencies. Figure Seven shows the NCC-related group that was earlier called the Foreign Mission Conference of North America, now the Division of Overseas Ministries of the National Council of Churches (the DOM). Also shown is the Interdenominational Foreign Mission Association (the IFMA), and the Evangelical Foreign Missions Association (E. F. M. A.) which is part of the National Association of Evangelicals. The growth of the latter two associations was not merely in the size of their member agencies. Together they had forty member agencies in 1946. By 1969 they had gained 64 to make 104, half of their members being new agencies that had been founded since the Second World War. There was also a total of 104 agencies in North America founded after the Second World War which, by 1970, had not become affiliated with any association whatsoever. When we take into account all of these figures, it would seem that Latourette's prophetic words quoted above had been fulfilled. By 1968 the initiative in fund raising and personnel recruitment was clearly in the hands of a host of new agencies. Almost all of these were in the cultural and theological tradition of the Evangelical Awakening and, for the most part, expressed their interests outside of the historic denominations.

Another new movement which sprang up in an unpredictable quarter, as prophesied by Latourette, was one which he himself very nearly overlooked. He was painfully aware that the Student Volunteer Movement had run its course as an agency for the recruitment of students for foreign missions. At Des Moines, Iowa in 1920, 6850 students attended the "Volunteer Convention" of the Student Volunteer Movement; 2783 signed decision cards indicating willingness to be foreign missionaries. In 1938, two years after he wrote the

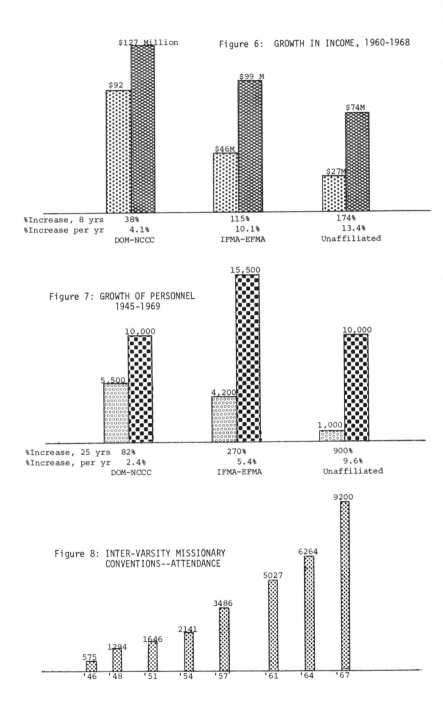

$127 Million   Figure 6: GROWTH IN INCOME, 1960-1968

$92

$99 M

$74M

$46M

$27M

%Increase, 8 yrs	38%	115%	174%
%Increase per yr	4.1%	10.1%	13.4%
	DOM-NCCC	IFMA-EFMA	Unaffiliated

Figure 7: GROWTH OF PERSONNEL
1945-1969

15,500

10,000

10,000

5,500

4,200

1,000

%Increase, 25 yrs	82%	270%	900%
%Increase, per yr	2.4%	5.4%	9.6%
	DOM-NCCC	IFMA-EFMA	Unaffiliated

Figure 8: INTER-VARSITY MISSIONARY
CONVENTIONS--ATTENDANCE

9200

6264

5027

3486

2141

1646

1294

575

'46 '48 '51 '54 '57 '61 '64 '67

prophetic words quoted above, only twenty-five signed cards. However, immediately following the Second World War, the Inter-Varsity Christian Fellowship began sponsoring a series of missions conferences for the purpose of challenging student involvement in foreign missions. The growth in attendance at these conferences is charted in Figure Eight. While attendance came to equal that of the quadrennial gatherings of the Student Volunteer Movement, it is difficult to compare the two organizations in regard to the number of cards signed indicating a willingness to serve overseas. The Inter-Varsity Christian Fellowship offered but did not urge them on the students, as had the SVM, but rather suggested that students take the cards home to think and pray about the matter if there were any doubt at all in their minds. There was consistent follow-up of mission interest, however, on the part of 2500 IVCF groups which met on college campuses. Between 1954 and 1969, 12,027 cards were signed, averaging out at about eight hundred per year and 2,400 per convention. It is interesting to note that even though the attendance at the conventions rose steadily to 9,200 in 1967, the number of cards signed per year during the whole period did not significantly change. This may mean that increased attendance did not in itself increase the number of students who through years of Christian background were prepared to make such a decision. More likely it simply reflected the deep-seated vocational uncertainty of college students.

Thus at the end of the period there was evident hesitance on the part of a younger generation that was apparently almost totally unaware of the extent of mission opportunity and expansion during the twenty-five years. For increase in financial resources, in personnel, and the sheer elaboration of organizational machinery --- in both Catholic and Protestant spheres --- no other period in history had displayed such an astonishing leap forward. Awakening in 1970 an observer from 1946 would have considered the story unbelievable.

The Turmoil in Mission Theory

The twenty-five unbelievable years also saw great strides in the formal Ecumenical Movement, which was able to bring almost all of the older Christian communions into the fellowship of the World Council of Churches. However, most of the new churches and mission agencies which were started by the new energies of the period were not immediately aware of the World Council of Churches. The many new dimensions of diversity were embarrasing at a time when concensus seemed near among churches that had for centuries stood aloof from each other. This impressive object lesson in unprecedented collaboration on the part of older churches seemed entirely lost on most of the new agencies. R. Pierce Beaver wryly commented on the fact that after decades of increasing collaboration between churches, dozens of agencies forced out of China began work in Taiwan without so much as tipping their hats to the Canadian Presbyterians who had a well-established work all over the island.[52] Although in this particular case the offense against the ecumenical ideal may have been committed as much by the older as well as by the newer agencies, nevertheless throughout the period it was the latter who were the most likely to begin new work where others had already labored and thus be the chief offenders against the logic of comity agreements. The feeling was that divisions back home were bad enough, and were like dirty laundry that should not be hung out in the view of the indigenous churches overseas. The Roman Catholic priest in a mountain town in Guatemala could not be consoled about the Protestant pluralism that invaded his parish and offered the people seven alternatives where formerly there was only one. Such people theorized that an indigenous national church would develop sooner and be confused less if there were only one alternative. They felt that the competition of foreign mission agencies or even national churches might encourage local people to reject them all and start their own indigenous movement or movements, only adding to the confusion. Yet, as Latourette so often reiterated, the multiform pattern of Protestantism admittedly encouraged great diversity, but also elicited the greatest overall response and allowed the deepest indigenous roots for the Christian faith.[53] It is possible that the essence of Christianity does not stand out so clearly when only one expression of it is available to view. But the problems of comity agreements and pluralism were only two of the many unresolved problems of mission theory that plagued most discussions on the nature of the church, and were by no means clarified at the end of the period.

One striking dimension in the discussion of mission theory was the feeling of some that any growth at all on the part of the institutional church was of questionable value. Such thinkers did not hail the origin and development of the many new agencies of the period. Not necessarily one of these, Van Leeuwen, in his provocative study, Christianity in World History, did suggest that something other than the organized church was unique in Western civilization and perhaps even more germaine to the concern of God.[54] For those to whom the extension of the church as an institution was not as impelling a Christian goal as the transformation of the world itself, evangelism had to be defined as any activity that would contribute to the wholesome development of society in accord with the will of God. Thus to this school of thought the implantation and growth of the institutional church came to be seen more and more as an affront to man-in-society and as an unnecessary accompaniment of the Christianization of the social order. This feeling was especially intense on the part of some of the church leaders in the developing countries, where continuing economic imperialism on the part of the missionary-sending countries seemed to retard the growth of national industry far more than mission efforts, directly and indirectly, could contribute to its development.

An element of irony could be seen here, in this situation in which church-produced leaders scorned the church, since it was the implantation and developing autonomy of a national church that had been the engine producing the very trained leaders which now had become so preoccupied with the transformation of the civil order that the institution of the church dwindled in significance in their eyes.

Thus the retreat from evangelism in favor of social action tended to arise precisely where mission work had long been established. The advance of communism and the resurgence of the non-Christian religions made well-trained second and third generation believers, whose consciences were caught up in the social currents of the time, feel that for the next few decades it would be expedient for the Christian mission to emphasize service, not conversion. While their conviction was shared by only a minority of Western missionaries and mission executives, these tended to be vocal and highly placed. As a result, the mission agencies related to these older "younger" churches sometimes became engrossed in comprehensive studies of the growth and development of a nation, rather than the growth and development of the church. On the other hand, as had been true with the older agencies in their youth, the social sensitivities of the newer agencies were more likely focused on immediate evils rather than the perverse structures of society, and were more likely centered on the salvation of the body and spirit of the individual rather than on the salvation---through revolution, if necessary---of the civil body politic.

This tension between evangelism and social action was wrongly reduced by some to a simple choice between "words" versus "deeds", when actually it was a question of words plus different kinds of deeds at different levels. Missionaries had always emphasized good deeds. William Carey initiated a movement that eventually resulted in the outlawing of widow burning in India. Robert Morrison and a host of other missionaries up until World War II opposed the custom of footbinding in China. And so on. Now, however, the novelty was a new and deeper awareness of the significance of the very structure of society itself as the object of the transforming power of Christ. Social change had become so rapid that many people for the first time became aware of the phenomenon of human organization. What was new was not the idea of rebuilding society---Christian personalities as divergent and as separated by history as Augustine, Thomas More, John Wesley, Livingstone, Noyes, and Rauschenbusch had all held radical views about the changes Christian faith must necessarily make by means of fundamental reform of society. What was new was that no longer just a few dreamers were involved: applied anthropology in Christian social concern had gained the prominence of a parlor game. The only danger was that at times the fundamental renewal of individuals was seen to be exclusively an effect, rather than also a cause, in the symbiosis between man and his culture.

At the same time, the traditional concept of mission was by no means abandoned. The great majority of churches,

national leaders, missionaries, mission executives and
mission boards pressed ahead in preaching the gospel to
every creature and in bringing individuals and families into
discipleship among the nations. The church in Korea grew
more in the years 1953-60 than it had in the previous sixty
years. The church in Sub-Sahara Africa more than tripled
from thirty to ninety-seven million. In Indonesia at least
fifty thousand Moslems became Christians---the first time
in history that such a turning from Islam had taken place.
The South India Conference of the Methodist Church in the
face of persecution grew from 95,000 to 190,000 members.
The Presbyterian Church in Taiwan between 1955 and 1965
engaged in a "Double the Church Campaign" and concluded it
successfully. In Latin America, largely due to ceaseless and
effective personal evangelism on the part of the Pentecostal
family of Churches, Protestants grew from about 1,900,000
in 1945 to at least 19,000,000 in 1970. In Brazil alone, by
1970, new congregations of the evangelical variety were being
founded at the rate of three thousand per year. Great campaigns of evangelism were undertaken during this period,
partly in response to the remarkable openness of many
populations to the Good News and partly as a determined
effort to counterbalance the new directions in mission being
advocated. Some campaigns were local, and confined to one
church or mission. Others, notably of the Evangelism in
Depth variety,[55] were nationwide, uniting many churches
and missions, and demonstrated the essential unity and cooperation of the Christian churches. Traditional church
growth was surveyed and studies published on many countries
---the Philippines, Congo, Liberia, Latin America, Mexico,
Brazil, Korea, Sierra Leone, Argentina, Ethiopia, Indonesia,
New Guinea, and other lands. The findings, though not as
often implemented as their authors hoped, helped focus
attention on old-fashioned evangelism and the multiplication
of self-supporting, self-governing, and self-propagating
churches.

   Thus the considerable turmoil in mission theory during
the period did not substantially change the long-standing
evangelical emphasis in Protestant missions except that the
basis of the support of the continued emphasis perceptibly
moved from the hands of older to new churches, and from

denominational back to interdenominational agencies. This gradual shift may be further illuminated by what was on the surface merely a discussion about the use of two words.

From Missions to Mission?

The concept of partnership in obedience highlighted at the International Missionary Council meeting at Whitby in 1947 acknowledged the relevance of national Christians as partners in the task of the missions working in their countries. But it was not until the 1952 meeting at Willingen that the sending countries became popularly recognized as mission fields in themselves. At that point there emerged a new sense of oneness in a single worldwide mission, and it seemed no longer reasonable that the International Missionary Council should concentrate on the task of missions in non-Western lands while the World Council of Churches concentrated on the unification of Christians in the Western world. Moreover, the increasing secularization in the West during the post World War II period brought into stark relief the need for evangelism and mission in the very backyard of the sending churches.

A prominent attempt to remedy the falseness of the dichotomy between the "Christian West" and "heathen lands" was the proposal to abandon the word missions in favor of a broader word mission.[56] The new term was meant to have greater breadth, both geographically and conceptually. It included Christian concern properly expressed in evangelism and Christian service in all parts of the world by all Christians from all lands, and it involved a mandate no less broad than the basic purposes of the church itself. Secondly, the new term was to refer to something quite different: the oneness of the mission, and therefore the appropriate oneness that ought to be expressed through collaboration in that mission. The concept of geographical breadth was thrilling and important, and was especially significant for those Christians who had thought of themselves as living in Christian lands while sending missions to heathen lands. In this sense, however, the new use of mission versus missions was not enthusiastically welcomed by Evangelicals, who from the time of the Evangelical Awakening had assumed that mission

began at the doorstep of the "believers' church" and that
every individual needed conversion, whether he was born
into a state church or a pagan tribe. There were already
hundreds of examples of widely supported interdenominational Evangelical mission projects inside the Western homeland. These ranged from the Pacific Garden Mission in
Chicago, reaching social dropouts, to the unique International
Christian Leadership, which sought conversions among
politicians, and was instrumental in the election of an Evangelical mayor of the city of Seattle, and, later on, an Evangelical
governor of the state of Washington. One agency, the Salvation Army, was very similar (except for celibacy) to a Catholic order, and specialized in conducting a mission to non-
Christians and unfortunates needing help within the Western
world; it also had work overseas. Toward the end of the
period, Teen Challenge was a Pentecostal effort that drew
on resources from many churches in an outstanding mission
to young people caught up in narcotics.

Many Christians were thus already using the old term
missions to refer to both the broader geographical and the
broader conceptual meaning now being proposed for mission.
Some denominations began using the term mission to refer
to whatever the church did. Local churches painted their
buildings with their "Local Mission" budget, and denominational headquarters rented their facilities with the "General
Mission" budget. The General Mission Budget became the
new name for a general purpose budget perhaps with the
hope that it would elevate those purposes. But at this point
many laymen were confused, especially those eager to donate
to agencies working in the "darkest situations", namely in
those lands where the number of Christians was minute.
Latourette himself was convinced that such lands demanded
priority. But the new use of mission covered what many considered both higher and lower priorities, and in any case
prevented supporters from making any such distinctions.

The second new emphasis for the term mission, which
had organizational implications, was in some ways equally
confusing. Five years after Willingen, at Ghana in 1957,
the International Missionary Council, in obedience to the
new vision, voted to merge with the World Council of
Churches. This proposal was accepted by the WCC at New

Delhi in 1961, and the first conference of the new WCC Commission of World Mission and Evangelism took place in Mexico in 1963. The meaningful title of the formal report of the Mexico meeting was "Mission in Six Continents" and, as it were, officially abolished once and for all the now out-dated idea that only one part of the world was mission territory. At no other meeting in history had so many dif-ferent Christian traditions been represented. For the first time Russian Orthodox representatives were present at a WCC meeting, having been voted in at New Delhi in 1961. For the first time representatives of "home mission" agencies gathered together with representatives of agencies formerly called "foreign missions." But the new "Unity in Mission" and the long-proposed "Joint Action for Mission" remained somewhat ambiguous:

> Lest we be misunderstood, we wish to say that Joint Action for Mission does not mean a simple pooling of resources, nor does it mean a redistribution of re-sources---a different sharing of the cake. Neither does it mean that every piece of work should be done jointly. It does mean that as Christ's mission is one, we dare no longer act as if it were as plural as are our churches and mission agencies.[57] (Italics mine.)

But if Joint Action for Mission did not mean literal, mono-lithic organizational unity in mission, how could several hundred agencies, undertaking to fulfill the Christian mission, no longer be referred to as missions? In the past, did the word missions necessarily imply that there was more than one Christian mission? The plural form of the word---missions---breathes decentralization and excitement, some-thing to challenge everyone. We need also a single term for all God wants done: the Christian mission. But the one does not have to take the place of the other.

The Councils and the Congresses

Remaining unclarified through all the discussion about mission and missions was the need to recognize two different dimensions of unity. The two dimensions of which we speak here are not organizational unity versus spiritual unity, which Mackay so significantly emphasized,[58] but rather two different dimensions of organizational unity. Why? The internal organization of the Christian people of God involves two radically different kinds of structures. The one is the churchly structure; the other is the kind of structure seen in a Catholic order or a mission society. The one is somewhat like a civil government; the other somewhat like a private enterprise. The achievement of unity in each dimension has been far easier than the unity of the two dimensions. That is, unity and cooperation between churchly structures has been relatively feasible, and correspondingly, cooperation between mission societies has been quite possible. But good understanding between the two dimensions---between churches and semi-autonomous mission societies (whether denominational or interdenominational)---has been in the Protestant tradition, very rare and difficult.

Curiously, a good deal of the impetus behind both the movement toward conciliar unity between churches, and the increasing trend to working unity between mission societies can be traced back to the famous 1910 World Missionary Conference in Edinburgh. That meeting was a "first" in eight significant ways, according to Latourette, number one of which was the fact that it was, more than any previous such gathering, "strictly a delegated body made up of official representatives of the missionary societies."[59] Still more curious is that sixty years later there had never been another gathering of that type and scope. Two streams sprang directly from the rock of that conference: 1) a series of conferences on "Faith and Order" and "Life and Work" which became the World Council of Churches, and, 2) a Continuation Committee of the conference itself which eventually became the International Missionary Council. But the Continuation Committee did not precisely continue nor attempt to repeat the kind of conference that had taken place in 1910. The 1910 conference was a representative body of mission agencies, including those which were interdenominational (e.g., controlled by church people, but not by churches as such), but the Continuation Committee eventually became a council "based upon bodies controlled by the churches,"[60]and finally a part of the WCC itself, as we have already seen. Interdenominational societies could not be directly represented with voting power as in 1910.

Meanwhile, the World Council of Churches, born officially in 1948, but in a real sense functioning since 1938, made giant strides during the twenty-five year period under discussion towards its objective of uniting all existing churchly structures into one loose yet formal organization, creating thereby, at the very minimum, a forum for sincere discussion of differences. In early 1970 some felt sure that soon the Roman Catholic Church would become a member. But structurally the WCC was an association of churches as churches. The meaning of the word church here was simply a community based on nuclear families, professing Jesus Christ as Lord, and organized by some kind of formal government. The characteristic church structure was a quasi-municipal structure, a government parallel to---and in many cases borrowed from---the type of government serving a nation, tribe or tongue, a city, county, state, or country. These civil structures, however, obviously compare very little in internal design or modus operandi to the private enterprise structures in society. In the same way, neither do the church structures compare in internal design or function to the non-denominational mission societies. The Billy Graham Evangelistic Association, for example, would no more have been invited to the World Council of Churches, as a church, than would the General Motors Corporation have been invited to the United Nations as a state, even though General Motors employs many more people than the entire population of some nation-members of the United Nations.

Thus, churchly unity and unity in churchly mission were to some extent provided by a series of councils of churches and councils of church mission agencies which constituted the mainstream of the Ecumenical Movement. But did the mission of the church end with the emergence of a new sense of the mission of the official church agency? By 1970, as we have seen, there had appeared what seemed to be a resurgence of interdenominational agencies expressing Christian purpose and mission in a movement reminiscent of the so-called "benevolent empire" in the first third of the nineteenth century.

Not surprisingly, then, the Ecumenical drive for churchly unity began to be counterbalanced in the sixties by a series

of Congresses on Evangelism, which brought together people
from probably as wide a variety of communions as the plen-
ary sessions of the World Council of Churches. By early
1970 the original World Congress that had been held in
Berlin in 1966 had been followed by regional congresses in
East Asia, West Africa, North America, Latin America, and
the Philippines, with others scheduled for other sectors. The
question of whom to invite as participants was handled in
different ways in the various parts of the world, reflecting
the structural confusion that continued to exist. The congresses did not intend to represent organized church structures, but rather the various agencies specializing in the
varied tasks of evangelism. In some cases the secretaries
of evangelism of major church bodies were specifically
invited; in other cases local people well known for their interest in evangelism were asked to form ad hoc committees
which then selected delegates representing a broad spectrum
of the different communication media being used for evangelism, rather than a comprehensive spectrum of ecclesiastical traditions. The task of evangelism was conceived of as
the task of the church, and yet the type of agencies sponsoring these conferences and participating most actively in them
in most cases were not churchly structures at all, but the
type of Christian "private enterprises" we have mentioned
above, different from churches in structure, yet generally
manned by people loyal to their own church communions
as individuals. It would seem that the existence of these
Congresses was simply an insistence on the part of a major
segment of Christendom that the Christian movement consisted of more than church institutions alone.

Church, Mission and the Oikoumene

A profound structural problem lay unresolved for both the
council and the congress leaders. This was the confusion
about whom to invite, arising, according to one writer,[61] from
the lack of acquaintance in Protestantism with the two kinds
of structures constituting in a significant and essential way
the very warp and the woof of the Roman Catholic Church.
The Protestant Reformation eliminated, say, the woof, when
it abolished the type of structure represented by the Catholic

orders, These were the agencies in which membership was ostensibly voluntary, which were committed to specific goals, and which did not automatically include all the people of any clan or biological community. It was pointed out that Protestantism did not become substantially involved in mission until a similar type of structure---that of the mission "society"---came into use at the very end of the eighteenth century. Those early Protestant mission societies, although embarrassingly unrelated to denominational structures, were in one sense stunningly ecumenical as well as inter-denominational. In 1795, the London Missionary Society solemnly, but naively, proposed to plant churches in foreign lands "without exporting any... form of Church Order and Government... but (only) the Glorious Gospel of the blessed God."[62] Even later on, when the first societies came into being that were launched by ecclesiastical action, such denominational boards were still basically voluntary agencies that depended for their personnel upon an elite membership, and for their support on the designated gifts of a dedicated minority of the members of those communions. That is why, as we have seen, John Mackay classified the Protestant mission societies as "Protestant orders": they were comparable in structure not to churches but to the Catholic orders.

However, the merger in 1961 of the International Missionary Council and the World Council of Churches, opposed by Max Warren, General Secretary of the Anglican Church Missionary Society (CMS), implied to some that mission was legitimately the responsibility of only the church structures. Because of this perspective and the structural features it implied, the great interdenominational and international mission societies were not, and could not be, invited to Mexico in 1963. These societies, such as the China Inland Mission-Overseas Missionary Fellowship (CIM-OMF), the Sudan Interior Mission (SIM), the Andes Evangelical Mission (AEM), the International Fellowship of Evangelical Students (IFES), the African Inland Mission (AIM), the Wycliffe Bible Translators (WBT), and the Billy Graham Evangelistic Association, etc., together sent thousands of missionaries, spent millions of dollars, and expressed the vision and purpose of believers in dozens of countries and countless communions. Yet because they did not have a churchly structure, they tended to be outside the realm of the formal Ecumenical Movement. Perhaps it will be said that even had they been invited to the Mexico meeting, such organizations would not have sent representatives because they did not believe in the kind of structuring represented by the Ecumenical movement at that time. If this was true, the fact that they were in fact structurally by-passed must have given credence to their belief. They would have been invited to Edinburgh in 1910. Of course, there were also theological and cultural barriers to their inclusion, but these were certainly no greater than what already existed within the World Council of Churches.

Throughout the twenty-five-year period there were indications of increased tension between liberal and conservative, liturgical and evangelical, etc. But in addition to all the usual reasons advanced for this tension, it was apparent that there were structural factors as well: Protestants did not clearly understand that the Christian oikoumene had to include both mission society and church, rather than one or the other. Ironically, the Student Volunteer Movement, the Student Christian Movement, and the YMCA had not only provided the majority of the leaders in the development of the Ecumenical Movement, but had provided the kind of structural vehicle from within which those leaders were able to work; yet by 1970 the structural trend of the Ecumenical Movement had, it seemed, long outgrown the need for the voluntary society. However, those society structures provided the necessary mobility and catalytic power for a kind of honeybee cross-fertilization between church structures that no churchly structure was capable of performing. But, to change the metaphor, it was supposed that once the conciliar structure was built, the scaffolding of the voluntary society could come down. The YMCA and the American Bible Society still existed on the fringe of the WCC meetings, sending fraternal (non-voting) delegates, but that was their only relationship. Thus, even the Anglican Church Missionary Society (CMS) could no longer have direct representation in any WCC body.

Thus, by 1970 the word ecumenical had become associated irretrievably with churchly unity, not the unity of, nor the unity with, non-churchly agencies. Moreover, the kind of evolution from mission-centered to church-centered structures that took place on a world level ensued in individual countries. In the non-Western countries, for example, intermission conferences, that in India began as early as 1855, grew into national Christian councils in the twentieth century. As churches emerged in the mission lands and more national workers were present at these meetings, the structural dilemma presented itself. To make a long story short, the councils in the non-Western lands became more and more councils of churches, not of missions. Church-planting mission agencies in the spirit of Henry Venn were content to fade away as they saw their fledgling churches grow up and meet together in their stead. But the functional missions, like the American Bible Society or the Wycliffe Bible Translators, simply had no place in the new structure that emerged. Neither was the existence of national mission societies widely encouraged. It was assumed that churchly structures were not only primary, but sufficient.

A similar evolution from mission unity to church unity occurred in the United States. Just as missionaries on the field had been drawn together by their involvement in the Christian mission and brought churches after them, so the executives of mission agencies were drawn together in the sending countries, and brought their churches closer together as a by-product. The Foreign Missions Conference of North America was begun in 1893, and brought together representatives of a large majority of U.S. and Canadian mission agencies, many of which at this point in history were denominational. This association of representatives of different churches was a powerful stimulant in drawing together the churches that formed the Federal Council of Churches of Christ in America and later the National Council of Churches of Christ in the United States of America, and the FMCNA itself eventually became part of the NCC. Thus again what was once a conference of mission agencies became overshadowed and subordinate to a council of churches.

By 1970, the NCC's Division of Overseas Ministries (which derived from the Foreign Missions Council of North America) was theoretically open to membership and fellowship on the part of interdenominational agencies. But in great part due to its subordination to a council of churches, only $2\frac{1}{2}$ percent of the 10,000 missionary personnel under agencies affiliated either on a direct or associate basis to the DOM were sent out by interdenominational agencies, and the few interdenominational agencies that were still related to the National Council of Churches were, for the most part, precisely agencies that had come down in that relationship from the days when the Foreign Missions Conference of North America included more interdenominational missions. Significantly, only a single church-planting interdenominational agency remained. Even this exception was not due to an American structural perspective but was, in effect, a concession to the European Lutheran approach to missions since the Santal Mission was just the American board of a mission based in Norway. Once again the characteristically American attitude toward non-churchly agencies prevailed.

However, the concept behind the Greek word <u>oikoumene</u> was still useful, however unfulfilled. Although the derived form in English, <u>ecumenical</u>, had gained the specific connotation of churchly unity, as we have seen, the Greek term could still be taken to mean a whole civilization and all of its institutions, not just the governmental structures. This is why a strict transliteration of the word <u>oikoumenical</u> seemed to be useful in addition to the current use of the word <u>ecumenical</u>. In 1970 <u>ecumenical</u> stood for the unity of churches and, by extension, for fellowship and consultation between whatever mission boards were tied into the basic budget of those churches, while the phrase <u>oikoumenical unity</u> might designate a relationship including all the avowedly Christian organizations of whatever kind that made up the Christian movement. Such a relationship could be both formal and informal, but not necessarily more organic than is the relationship sustained by all the various private enterprises and governmental structures that are found in a non-socialistic society. Thus the Commission of World Mission and Evangelism of the World Council of Churches was quite ecumenical, in that its leadership derived from the World Council of Churches, which by definition was an <u>ecumenical</u> body. But the CWME was not composed (as was Edinburgh, 1910) of delegates from mission agencies, both denominational and interdenominational, and its membership did not even represent directly the agencies belonging to the member churches. This fact, of course, was the result of the demise of the International Missionary Council, which, as we have noted, had been related primarily to National Christian Councils around the world, which unlike councils of churches included mission agencies as such.

Structurally different was the Vatican II council, which could be called oikoumenical since it seated as voting delegates not only the territorial bishops of the church, but also representatives of Catholic orders such as the Jesuits, Dominicans, Franciscans, etc. Also by contrast was the Evangelical Foreign Missions Association, which in 1969 was probably the most oikoumenical mission-oriented body of its size, since its representatives came from mission agencies (not churches) that were both denominational (70%) and interdenominational (30%). Closer collaboration between the Interdenominational Foreign Mission Association and the Evangelical Foreign Missions Association also began to develop in the sixties (the first joint conference of executives took place in 1967) and was producing an even larger and more oikoumenical body than the EFMA alone.

By this definition, then, the series of Congresses on Evangelism could have been described as oikoumenical, not merely ecumenical, but they were so in varied degrees, with no clear definitions of structure. But something was emerging. A second Congress on Evangelism was being planned for 1971. However, would there ever be another conference like Edinburgh, 1910? The only worthy successor would be a representative, deliberative assembly calling together all the Christian agencies in the world devoted to the evangelization of the world, whether denominational or interdenominational, whether Western or non-Western, whether national or international, whether church-planting, church-building, or church-serving. Who should sponsor such a conference? For the World Council of Churches to do it would perhaps be like the United Nations taking over the planning for the World's Fairs. Did the Christian movement need its own "World's Fair"? Certainly a man from Mars would learn more about the human race at a World's Fair than at a meeting of the United Nations since the World's Fair draws together both

public and private enterprises of all sorts, both the warp and
the woof of human civilization. Could a man from the secular city learn more about the people of God at a Christian
conference of that kind than at a World Council of Churches
meeting? It is not to be doubted. Who has ever summed up
the thousands of different enterprises that serve the distinctive interests and needs of the oikoumenical church (e.g.
Christianity as a movement, a people of God)?

Somehow the vast array of diverse organisms within the
body of Christ must be better understood than was possible
in early 1970. Only as a harmonious, corporate whole does
the full reality of Christianity appear, and only then will the
mission of the people of God be correctly understood in relation to the various missions expressing that mission---
missions that are as small as an individual seeking to obey
his living Lord, a group of two or three gathered together,
a parish task force, a para-church structure, a denominational agency, and interdenominational agency, a council of
churches, an association of pastors, an association of agencies of a given type, a congress, a world church festival.
Between 1945 and 1970 the unbelievable years had made one
thing utterly certain: the ever-unfolding diversity and complexity of the Christian movement had not outgrown its one
mission nor its many missions. The truly oikoumenical
reality of the Christian movement could no longer be de-
limited.

5

PREPARATION FOR

TOMORROW

Christianity is certainly concerned as much about tomorrow as about yesterday. Dr. Latourette was a master of the facts of tomorrow, but also well illustrates in his writings the value of that kind of knowledge for an understanding of what is yet to happen. His book, Missions Tomorrow, written in 1936 before the beginning of the Second World War, was a trenchant analysis of the differences between nineteenth and twentieth century missions and predicted with astonishing accuracy the new trends in missions in the period to follow. In 1947, following the conference at Whitby, which itself followed that final mammoth internal convulsion through which the Western world passed prior to its Great Retreat, he and William Richie Hogg spoke again of "tomorrow" in their book, Tomorrow is Here. The "tomorrow" of those writings was, to a great extent, our period of the twenty-five unbelievable years. The "tomorrow" has now passed, and in early 1970 the world faces still another. It is a world torn by racial strife, weary in morale, uneasy about traditional morality, unprecedentedly wealthy in some sectors yet massively hungry and destitute in others, and in some ways more sobered and more mature. It is like a youth who has finally gained his college diploma only to discover that the great issues and problems of his lifetime are still ahead of him.

The Shape of Tomorrow

Any serious preparation for tomorrow must take into account the novelties of its shape. From the viewpoint of early 1970 it will be necessary to try to avoid well-known virtual certainties which hardly need mentioning and remote possibilities that hardly deserve mentioning. This leaves several aspects of the shape of tomorrow that merit attention.

One aspect would certainly be the phenomenon of the "passing of the torch." The process has already begun. In the United Nations General Assembly the votes of the non-Western nations are already clearly the majority. It seems logical that the same thing can happen in the World Council of Churches and in any other gathering intended to represent the whole world, either secular or Christian. Sheer brute force measured in stock piles of atomic weapons or magnitude of technological capacity may remain a Western monopoly for some time to come. However, the very gap between the rich nations and the poor nations, whether measured in terms of material wealth or technological and scientific competence, tends in itself to introduce an unstable factor into the picture. Now that the production of nuclear weapons is no longer exclusively a Western skill, the total quantity of such bombs is not so important; old formulas of power politics no longer apply, and it seems increasingly necessary for Western nations to deal politely with non-Western nations, regardless of the latter's industrial capacity or political maturity. Likewise, in the world of missions the mere balance of financial power is determinedly considered irrelevant in a great many of the new relationships between sister churches.

A second factor to reckon with is the increasing acceptability of neo-pietist or Pentecostal elements of worship and fellowship. In early 1970 it appears that the Pentecostal movement may easily become as influential and permanent a contribution to the historic Western Christian tradition as has been the Evangelical Awakening. The Pentecostal movement was born in an age when an emotional ingredient in Christian worship was not as vehemently rejected as it was in the days of the Evangelical Awakening. Also the role of women in the secular world had drastically changed, and the new Pentecostal movement built upon the current attitude, granting women a more important role in the church than any other major movement. Pentecostalism will lead the way in the actual practice of the Reformation dictum of the priesthood of all believers. The charismatic movement will produce a greater sensitivity to the natural gifts present in the congregation. Other churches outside of the specifically Pentecostal tradition will partake indirectly of the increasing humanization of the Christian tradition. But that which is added on peripherally to the older churches will be built into the very structure of the Pentecostal churches.

Many other traits of tomorrow will in one way or another involve changes in structure. Both unification and diversification will take place. Both centralization and decentralization are processes that will be active, the latter perhaps more than the former. The village church in some countries will become more and more only a memory---at least in the sense whereby the same people were involved as a community in the locus of their work, their social relationship, and their worship. In many a non-Western land the urban population will soon outstrip the rural. The urban church will eventually master the task of providing vocational, social, and residential modules so that the "multi-valent" man of the new urban world may become more fully Christian than the romanticized village Christian of a former era. This new kind of Christian will have a more profound effect upon society than at earlier times. The family will become more visible as a Christian structure. There may even be "larger families" of Christians living in common commitment whose structure will be halfway between the "believers' church" and the Catholic order. Premonitions of this type of structure are already seen in the secular monasticism of Synanon, a disciplined community built out of people who have been rehabilitated from drug addiction. The earlier pattern long seen in the Salvation Army might become more common in the future, should the genius of its operation become more widely understood. At the opposite extreme there will be churches in increasing numbers in which there will be no formal membership as such.

Structure as Servant or Master?

More than ever, the shape of tomorrow will be the result
of the conscious design and remodeling of structures rather
than gradual, unintentional development. A century of ama-
teurish and merely intuitive groping characterized the Age
of Revolution in the Marxian period in regard to the conscious
modification of the structures of society. But in the new
period, first in business and industrial circles, and then
finally in civil and ecclesiastical spheres, a much matured
systems engineering, sophisticated by additional insights
from anthropology, sociology, and social psychology, will
enable a much more effective reevaluation of church structures, denominational and local.

The cross-cultural, overseas mission structures will also
come under review and evaluation at the same time, perhaps
even in advance of home church organizations. Because the
overseas mission agencies have had to work with many con-
trasting cultures simultaneously, a certain kind of structural
sophistication has often resulted. This does not mean that
they have not made mistakes, but both because of and in spite
of their errors, the insight of churchmen with overseas experience has been salutary when complex issues have been
faced by Western churches. However, they have not solved
all the problems overseas. For example, mission agencies
have typically worked themselves out of jobs. As a national
church develops in a non-Western country, the mission generally assumes that the church should increase and that
therefore the mission must decrease. But the structure be-
comes the master rather than the servant if the church-
planting mission maintains the prerogative of power too long
or by subtle pressures---financial or otherwise---continues
to make the crucial decisions. Perhaps it is too simple a
solution, however, for the mission to be dismantled and its
personnel loaned to a sister church in another country. Since
both the sending and the receiving churches retain their autonomy, neither should be limited in its mission outreach by
the unique visions of the other, even within the same country.
Perhaps through structural remodeling a new kind of agency
can be established which will retain the mobility and initiative of the paternalistic mission, yet neither be supervisory

nor competitive to the younger church, nor even necessarily structurally related to it in any way.

Considerable remodeling may also be necessary to develop more dialogue between corresponding aspects of home and foreign mission structures, especially those operated by the same denomination. For example, discussion is going on at an unofficial level in the United Presbyterian Church concerning the possibility of forging a direct relationship between the different departments of home mission in the United States and the corresponding departments of home mission in the younger Presbyterian churches overseas. This would remedy the illogic of the home board of missions dealing with the Navajo Indians in the United States and the overseas board dealing with Mayan Indians in Mexico without any communication between the two operations. Similarly, university work in Mexico City is conducted by the overseas department of the church, and yet another department of the same U.S. denomination conducts work on university campuses in the United States. Or one department of the church is struggling with Spanish Sunday School lessons for Latin America, while another department faces the necessity of doing something for Spanish churches in the United States. Collaboration is beginning, but restructuring could make it automatic.

Restructuring is looming up as regional and local administration of mission on the home front are more and more conceived of as a replacement for a home-mission board based in national denominational offices. A regional approach to mission is in fact one of the chief features of the Consultation on Church Union (COCU). Within existing denominations hundreds of local mission projects (like coffee houses) have emerged recently, some of them interdenominational, that tend to divert funds that would otherwise reach the denominational mission agencies on the national level. Closely allied to this problem is the matter of trying to raise funds for a conglomerate budget. Rightly or wrongly, church people are less and less inclined to give to a comprehensive budget and then to hope to influence the use of that budget afterwards. Their voting power has perhaps irretrievably gravitated from the level of the formal process of budget formation to the moment in which the act of giving occurs.

Structural remodeling may sometimes produce simpler

structures, but more likely will result in more complicated ones. An example is the Evangelism-in-Depth program originated by the Latin America Mission.[63] It is a unique, catalytic structure whose expertise consists of the ability to "orchestrate" what are otherwise independent churches and Christian agencies in a region or country. Distantly derived from this movement is the New Life for All structure in Nigeria, which though a tiny operation in terms of staff, has had an immense and continuing influence on the well-being of the Christian movement in that country. This sort of structure may be the wave of the future. Another form of integration which is needed and may appear is the type of world oikoumenical festival which was mentioned in the last section. This will take considerable structural remodeling, again more likely greater elaboration than simplification.

Strategic Consultation

The world church exists, but it is not yet knitted together by sufficient internal consultation. The establishment of Evangelical Missions Information Service, which constitutes the emergence of formal, continuous liaison between the Interdenominational Foreign Mission Association (IFMA) and the Evangelical Foreign Missions Association (EFMA), has been both the cause and the effect of a good deal of strategic consultation. The first major joint project of IFMA and EFMA was the Wheaton Congress on the Church's Worldwide Mission. Already the Evangelical Missions Quarterly (EMQ) had appeared. Then came the Evangelical Committee for Latin America (ECLA) and the Committee to Assist Missionary Education Overseas (CAMEO). In 1968 CAMEO brought together a hundred key people from all over the world to study ministerial preparation by extension education. Later it sold over one thousand copies of a six-hundred-page book reporting on the extension movement.[64] With the constantly increasing possibilities of consultation between people and agencies involved in similar mission tasks, there is an increasing awareness of the selfhood of the world Christian community. There are already communications conferences, literature conferences, radio conferences, writers' conferences, Sunday School conferences, Church

Growth conferences, and conferences drawing together leaders in theological education. One organization, the WCC's
Theological Education Fund, contributed effectively to the
development of regional associations of theological schools.
Another, World Vision, Inc., has convened more than seventy
national pastors' conferences in the non-Western lands, involving over fifty thousand men. Such strategic consultation
will very likely increase. Coordination is the essential practical purpose. Beaver's words are appropriate:

Protestantism needs to find through voluntary association some common organ for planning and action similar
in function, but not in authority, to the Roman Catholic
Sacred Congregation for the Propagation of the Faith.
Through it, when found, the common effort may be demo-
cratically guided without destroying the vitality and zeal
of the hundreds of separate units. Somehow the dangers
of remoteness, uniformity, and irresponsibility inherent
in centralization must be avoided, and every last local
congregation and individual disciple, as well as each
denomination, be brought into real and direct participation.[65]

Who knows what will become of Edwin Espy's proposal
for the restructuring of the National Council of Churches
in the United States.[66] In part it is a proposal to decentral-
ize, and many new agencies may spring into existence, such
as OPRO (Overseas Personnel Recruitment Office) which
is already actively at work, although only eight denominations are behind it; other churches may begin to use its
services unofficially. There was a time when this kind of
thing was frowned on in the name of conciliar unity, but by
1970 function was beginning to be more important than
rigid adherence to simplistic concepts of church order.

Another aspect[*] of consultation is the efficient use of the
printed page. A conference can initiate discussion about an
important issue. But books, even books without pictures,
although not as emphatic or impressive a medium of communication as face-to-face consultation, do provide a remarkably low cost, compact, and efficient means of review
and random access to facts and discussions about which the
reader is already motivated.

However, most of the many necessary specialized books

to fuel the fires of reevaluation and new approach have not yet broken into print. The reason is, in great part, the lack of established markets to finance them. Only a market can justify the printing of a book. But consultation is both the cause and the effect of the printed page. Most publishers of religious books do not seek to serve small, specialized markets. Apparently a host of new one-room "satellite" publishers are needed,[67] whose primary skill will be the identification of a specific, specialized market, and the employment of outside commercial facilities for the printing, and newsletters to specialized circles for the means of publicity. This presumes the prior existence of myriads of specialized newsletters.

Documents that merely sum up one man's analysis of a problem and go from him to others are a one-way communication. Yet, consultation requires something more than one-way newsletters or one-way books. There must be feedback and an on-going conversation. The sense of finality with which we often regard a book must be a thing of the past. Revised editions must be more frequent and must incorporate conversation-in-reply to earlier editions. Books and newsletters must be part of a two-way on-going conversation.

There are two kinds of institutions that can greatly contribute to the quantity and quality of strategic consultation in the Christian movement. One is the center for advanced studies. The Christian movement has grown far faster than the academic centers related to it. For example, in many fields the annual need for additional pastoral leaders on the congregational level is at least ten times the capacity of formal training facilities to prepare them. In Brazil alone there are 3,000 new churches a year, with hardly more than one tenth that many ministers graduating per year. But the situation is even worse in regard to the facilities for the advanced training of cross-cultural missionary personnel. It is said that there are five thousand such workers in the United States home on furlough in any given year, yet there was in 1970 only one school in the United States with a multiple staff geared primarily for the advanced (not candidate) training of cross-cultural Christian workers.[68] Such schools must be multiplied.

Another essential contribution to consultation is the kind

of agency represented by the Missions Advanced Research and Communication Center (MARC).[69] Its staff of systems engineers and computer experts produce for the Missionary Research Library (at Union Theological Seminary, N.Y.) the Directory of North American Protestant Ministers Overseas, and are working in a similar capacity on the 1971 edition of the World Christian Handbook, which is being greatly improved and expanded. Somewhat similar in the Roman Catholic sphere is the International Federation of Institutes for Social and Socio-Religious Research (FERES). A new research organization, Daystar Communications, Inc.[70] is a team of professional researchers utilizing the human life sciences to test and conduct projects of research in the growth and development of the Christian church. These organizations are very new, yet are already staggering under the load of even the rudimentary work of this type that needs to be done as the Christian movement faces the seventies.

What is the Goal?

As the whole family of man increasingly participates in a worldwide Christian community, the personalities of each member of that family will make their own contribution in their own way. As we prepare for tomorrow it will be difficult but essential for the Western world to understand the fact that the institutional shape of its own particular life in Christ is authentic but partial. The expansion of Christianity into the non-Western world is not merely the extension of a Western variety of that faith, but is the stirring of the other members if a world family into life and fellowship. It is as though a philharmonic orchestra had been broken up and scattered across the earth, and each section of musical instruments had lost its ability to play in concert with the other instruments, and even the skills in each section had fallen into decay. But then, one by one, the instruments are redeemed and brought into concert again. To join the reunited orchestra the sections do not need to abandon their particular instruments, but precisely must be encouraged to utilize them as their distinctive contribution. Some instruments are more numerous than others; there is radical diversity and potentially chaos in the warm-up period. But with a

single, divinely-given musical score to unite them, there
will issue forth a sound which no man has ever heard before,
which is far more than the sum of parts, a heavenly sound
that will grow in the splendor and glory of God as each new
instrument is added.

In 1970 there was no guarantee that this process, so strik-
ingly furthered during twenty-five unbelievable years, would
continue. But at least the record did not support the widespread pessimism of the period. Like the disciples of old,
the Christians of 1970 did not know the times and seasons
of their Lord's return. But they could obey with confidence
the King's command, "Occupy until I come."

It is a tribute to the insight and faith of Latourette that
his characteristic realism-optimism, expressed in 1936, is
even more appropriate at the end of the period we have
called "The Twenty-Five Unbelievable Years."

The new day is one of confusion. Many have lost a
sense of direction and purpose. They are terrified by
the passing of the old and familiar and by specters of
disaster in the path ahead. It is the great privilege of
Christians to discover a fresh vision of the high calling
of God in Christ Jesus, to declare, from conviction born
through struggle, doubt, despair---and faith and exper-
ience--- that human life and history have meaning, that
men are not orphans in a chaotic and cruelly indifferent
universe, but have open before them the possibility of a
growing and endless fellowship with the God and Father
of our Lord Jesus Christ... The great "good news," the
gospel of Christ, is that God is not dead, but that He
lives, that He is the great fact of the universe and of
human experience, that the Eternal God, the Creator,
loves men and seeks to transform them, to win them to
fellowship with Himself and to build them into a new
community, both present and future, a community of
this present world and of the world to come, a community embracing the noble souls of all ages and lands and
climes. It is our high privilege in this day which we are
entering to join in the vision of that community and to
share with God and with those who have gone before us
in carrying it one stage further toward its consummation.
We can work in confidence that He will take whatever in

our weakness and our ignorance we attempt to do for Him and multiply it many fold and bring it to fruitage in a far more glorious, even though in a different fashion than we have ever dared to dream.

"Now unto him that is able to do exceedingly abundantly above all that we ask or think, according to the power that worketh in us, unto him be glory in the church by Christ Jesus throughout all ages, world without end. "[71]

Appendix

THE MAN AND THE ISSUE

A

THE RELUCTANT MISSIONARY

An encounter with the police was the first thing that happened to this boy from Oregon when he arrived at Yale: "I had saved money by not going Pullman," Latourette recalled the experience. "I had some rough nights on the train, and after riding day coaches, I was desperately tired. I came to the (New Haven) Green, stretched out on the grass, and a policeman ordered me to get up."

He already had a record. He had previously been "apprehended" by officials of the Student Volunteer Movement. Of that event he said:

"I felt as if I had signed my death warrant. I hadn't the slightest desire to be a missionary. I hated the thought, but it seemed to be a clear duty."

This boy was destined to become a very unusual man. Unusual in unusual ways. Not a brash platform type, a "bookish lad," he was the last to want to go to China. One day Director of Graduate Studies at Yale, never married, he lost his faith after becoming a professor, was kidded for preaching a sermon in his inaugural address as president of the American Historical Society.

This is not the half of it. Many seminary professors have not yet come to grips with his major insight, though he produced for them a scholarly book a year for the last fifty-two years. His latest book is not yet off the press, and another is only half finished.

A few months ago---the day after Christmas---the boy on the Green, now an old man dressed in a dark suit, was knocked down on the highway. His last evening walk.

Student power made him. It was the Student Volunteer Movement, the SVM, most influential student movement in history. It moved pell-mell through the Ivy League schools and raced across the States. It reached Kenneth Scott Latourette in Oregon.

"I remember pacing the beach night after night, struggling with the problem." His parents' friends were aghast at his decision. He was not himself overjoyed.

"The last honorable thing I wanted to be was a missionary."

He had to learn Greek entirely on his own. He packed off to Yale, and---after getting up off the grass---finished in one year (his western college training was solid). Student leaders decided he should go to China. To work under the 'Yale-in-China' educational mission he completed his doctorate, pioneering in Far Eastern studies. Now finally he had to make good on his SVM commitment made five years earlier.

"I think if anybody had told me even on the day I sailed that it was all off, that I needn't go out, I would have thrown up my hat and given three cheers... I must say that when I did arrive and came to know my colleagues and began to be familiar with China, I was profoundly grateful that I was there."

It was a long trip and a short story. One year in China was followed by eight months of dysentery, the kerosene treatment... and two years of recovery in Oregon. Now he taught at two colleges and was called to Yale to take the chair of missions.

Student power? As a graduate student at Yale, he didn't drum up all alone those Bible study groups that drew a thousand students. He merely carried through faithfully in a movement much larger than he. Indeed, he had no business at Yale otherwise. He was out of place. His point of contact, his roots, were in the Student Volunteer Movement and what it was doing on campus. He hung his hat at Yale, never quite feeling at home. But he went, and he stayed, because this was where he felt he could best serve.

Poring over his autobiography, <u>Beyond the Ranges</u>, you are in another world. Here is a man in a movement where "to do your own thing" is to dishonor the Christ Who asked a man to do His thing. But, like Wesley, neither his willingness to cross an ocean nor his disciplined daily devotions solved all his problems. After becoming professor of missions, his faith waned and his health broke.

"I had come to see something of the seamy side of ecclesiastical and official religious life and found myself wondering whether Christianity was confirmed by its fruits."

This was more serious than the China dysentery. This time it was more spirit than body. But God answered. He returned to his chair at Yale on a higher spiritual plane. His next forty years of service became his most productive. Still the quiet retiring bachelor, he became "Uncle Ken" to countless students who today constitute a family that circles the globe. He answered mimeographed letters with handwritten notes.

He continued to play a leading role in Far Eastern Studies, even in the secular sphere (during twenty years he taught all the courses Yale offered on the Far East), and his chair was amplified to "Professor of Missions and Oriental History." The faculty wanted to make it "Oriental History and Missions" but he knew which he wanted first. His writings on the Chinese set an example in appreciative objectivity and scientific method.

He had no dull moments. His thoughtful manner, his immense erudition, his quiet Christian commitment and his willingness to be of service landed him on many a board of directors of an active Christian cause. For years he spent a full day each week in New York in this service.

"At the height of my folly, I was serving on thirty-three boards and committees in New York and New Haven, including four mission boards."

But the field of his greatest endeavor and his most unique influence has to do with all those books. Not the Far Eastern Studies—we'll come back to those. It's those 10,000 printed pages of books and articles he wrote about the story of Christianity.

But it's not how much he wrote. That alone, of course, is little short of a miracle (when added to his students, his classes, his boards and committees). Rather it is what he wrote that astounds.

In the first place, this kid from Oregon was not tempted to write from a European point of view. He was culturally an outsider---even in New Haven, I suspect, and surely to the internal quarrels of European history and theology. He was the first man to undertake the whole story of the Christian movement.

"The founders of the Bay Colony in Massachusetts get little more preferential treatment than those who brought the faith to the Belgian Congo," writes biographer Wilber Harr.

It may have been significant that Oregon, in the nineteenth century, had a great deal to do with Canton. Is China more important than Europe? Not only did he describe Christianity wherever he found it, but he described all kinds of Christianity with a sympathetic and scientific objectivity that sometimes blanched partisans of specific traditions. He was the first scholar to give Protestants, Roman Catholics, Orthodox and Nestorians equal time.

Even more disturbingly, he believed you could write the story of Christianity simply as a historian. One wonders if his unconfessed secret was the belief that the lack of theology was an advantage, not a handicap. If so, he never said so, and never would have said so. But here is one tangible gap in his credentials: he did not undergo the customary orientation of seminary theological studies. Neither the SVM nor the Baptists made such a requirement. Some people never quite forgave him for getting a Ph. D. in history instead of a B. D. But getting a B. D. is not the sort of thing you can go back and do over again, certainly not after you have been appointed dean of graduate studies in a divinity school.

The whole life of Latourette is in effect a kindly but formidable onslaught upon the religious establishment. The fact of this loyal opposition has curiously been disguised by his innate humility and genuine commitment to Christ as Lord. Here is not a rebellious, destructive critic but a profoundly constructive citizen. It might be said that his primary loyalty was to Christ rather than His Church. Organizations, even the "Church," were means, not ends. This is due in part to his Baptist inheritance and in part to his long and intense association with the Student Volunteer Movement which impatiently pushed past the slow-moving church structures of its day.

He was a reluctant missionary: he would have preferred to stay home. He was a reluctant professor; his "primary concern was students, not a subject." He was a reluctant churchman; the vast bulk of his labors was related to non-churchly structures like the SVM, the YMCA, the WSCF, the JICU, and Yale itself. He was a reluctant Easterner; he would have preferred to stay at Denison where the students "were the sort of boys I had been reared with... I went to the Yale faculty from a sheer sense of duty." He was the reluctant evangelical; his honesty led him though deep waters of agnosticism, but deeper experience confirmed him in evangelical faith.

He was not reluctant about his convictions. Of interest to missionary strategists today is his attitude toward "group conversion," which he was willing to endorse in spite of a good deal of contrary opinion. The fact that he believed Matthew 28:19 contains the "very words" of our Lord as He gave His followers the Great Commission greatly influenced his theory and theology of mission. Missionary experience in China and Baptist convictions predisposed him to favor the "one by one against the social tide" mode of becoming Christian, but his encyclopedic knowledge of how churches have multiplied on new ground led him to believe that group conversion was not only valid but desirable.

"More and more, we must dream of winning groups," he wrote in Missions Tomorrow (Harper, 1936.) "Too often... we have torn men and women, one by one, out of the family, or village, or clan, with the result that they have been permanently de-racinated and maladjusted... it is much better if an entire natural group... can come rapidly over into the faith."

Thus when Bridges of God by McGavran appeared in 1954, advocating the people movement mode of discipling the peoples of the earth, Latourette gladly wrote the Foreword, saying:

"Here is a book which boldly sets forth the issue and makes positive and sweeping proposals for a change... one of the most important books on missionary methods that has appeared in many years."

Latourette agreed to be one of the sponsors of the Institute of Church Growth which was established at Eugene,

Oregon in 1963. After the Institute of Church Growth was incorporated into the new School of World Mission at Fuller Theological Seminary, Dr. McGavran, now dean of this new enterprise, invited him to give the 1971 Church Growth Lectures on the subject of European People Movements. The topic was proposed because of the widespread misunderstanding afflicting world evangelization that Christianity was a good religion until---after Constantine---the Church began to take in multitudes. Latourette believed, on the contrary, that (a) history proved that the great people movements to Christ of A.D. 300-1000 were the only way in which European populations could have been won, and (b) they are today and tomorrow a valid and valuable way to disciple the nations. Consequently, on December 5, 1968, he wrote agreeing to deliver six lectures on European People Movements. His tragic death three weeks later made it impossible for him to carry out his intention. Thus it remains for someone else to illuminate the future of world evangelization by portraying the significant part people movements have played in the past.

He was not reluctant in regard to the will of Christ, nor the love of Christ for China. It was as if he foresaw the shifting of the world's center of gravity to China. More than anything else---from his home in Oregon and its ties to Canton---he set his heart upon China. He came back from China, but he did not turn his back on China. He is popularly known for his unequaled historical treatment of the whole sweep of Christianity. Even these monumental labors can be seen as part of the broadest possible tooling-up for China. China was the basic challenge, to him, to us. China still is.

Yes, we misunderstand Kenneth Scott Latourette if we think of him merely as historian, or as church historian. Evangelical scholars will wonder how in the final years of maximum insight and experience he could take the time to "revise thoroughly" (his own words) a secular treatment of China. China is the reason. God called him first to. China and secondarily to that, to the study of all Christian history. Some say that he beautifully rounded out his career, and that his death did not tragically cut off anything that was unfinished. In a literal sense, perhaps, but in an existential sense, no. China remains. China is unfinished. The people of China must yet express in their own way "the light of the glory of God in the face of Jesus Christ." KSL, the reluctant missionary, has shown us the way. What a refreshing thing to reflect on KSL in an age that glamorizes individual freedom. His greatness did not pop out of a free use of freedom. Naked obedience, against the strong currents of personal preference, was the basis of all the key decisions of his life. Here was a man reborn in joy and sustained in delight in the will of God because he was willing again and again for "sheer duty" to overcome human reluctance. (Reprinted by permission of *World Vision Magazine*)

1929 A History of Christian Missions in China
1936 Missions Tomorrow
1937-44 A History of the Expansion of Christianity
    Vol. 1: The First Five Centuries
    Vol. 2: A Thousand Years of Uncertainty
    Vol. 3: Three Centuries of Advance
    Vol. 4: The Great Century: Europe and the USA.
    Vol. 5: The Great Century: The Americas, Australasia, Africa
    Vol. 6: The Great Century: Northern Africa and Asia
    Vol. 7: Advance Through Storm
1940 Anno Domini: Jesus, History and God
1946 The Gospel, the Church and the World
1948 The Christian Outlook
1948 Tomorrow is Here (With Wm. Richey Hogg)
1949 The Emergence of a World Christian Community
1949 Missions and the American Mind
1950 These Sought a Country
1953 A History of Christianity (1500 pages)
1954 The Christian Mission in Our Day
1955 Challenge and Conformity
1957 World Service (A History of the YMCA Overseas)
1958-62 Christianity in a Revolutionary Age
    Vol. 1: The Nineteenth Century in Europe:
        Background and Roman Catholic Phase
    Vol. 2: The Nineteenth Century in Europe:
        Protestant and Eastern Churches
    Vol. 3: The Nineteenth Century Outside Europe:
        Americas, Pacific, Asia, Africa
    Vol. 4: The Twentieth Century in Europe:
        Roman Catholic, Protestant and Eastern Churches
    Vol. 5: The Twentieth Century Outside Europe
1960 Frontiers of the Christian World Mission
1965 Christianity Through the Ages
1968 Behind the Ranges

Figure 9: SELECTED BOOKS BY LATOURETTE

B

THE TAPESTRY OF

THE CHRISTIAN STORY

The list of books on the opposite page is illustrative of the way in which Latourette's writings constitute a tapestry of the Christian story.

In 1929 appeared his lengthy work on Christian Missions in China. This confirmed his special interest in China. But his very next book was on the worldwide Christian movement, and appeared as a study book in 1936 looking forward to the meetings of the International Missionary Council at Madras. Ringing with insight, there is almost nothing about it that is no longer relevant. It needs in fact to be reissued; it has been cited several times in our essay on the Twenty-Five Unbelievable Years.

But his two largest works are also worldwide in scope. We all stand indebted to Zondervan for deciding to reissue them. The basic tapestry (to 1944) is the earlier, seven-volume <u>A History of the Expansion of Christianity</u>. The later, five-volume <u>Christianity in a Revolutionary Age</u> does not revise or retrace but supplements the 1815-1962 period, giving a great deal of extra material on the European churches as well as a wealth of additional material on Christianity in the United States. The chart following shows the relationships between these two multi-volume works.

It would seem quite feasible for Christian colleges to utilize these two sets of books as the historical backbone of an education in the liberal arts. That is how comprehensive they are. Rather than trying to add a Christian supplement to some secular work which grossly down-plays or completely ignores the role of the Christian movement in Western Civilization, it might be better to let the Christian movement be the backbone of Western Civilization---as it really was---and supplement this story with secular accounts where necessary. It would be possible, for example, for the seven-volume set to be used for the first-year college course on Western Civilization. Then the second-year course on U.S. history could be built around the 670 pages of material on the United States found in the two sets. Many other courses could also lean against the historical tapestry provided by these twelve books.

Dr. Latourette's other books condense these larger works (e.g. 1940, 1965), or highlight special themes (e.g. 1946, 1949, 1950, 1955, 1957), or summarize the existing situation with a look into the future (1948, 1954, 1960). One book (1968) is autobiographical, and it was published just before he died, in December 1968. A superb brief account of his life is to be found in Wilbur Harr's Frontiers of the Christian World Mission Since 1938, a book which also includes an informal autobiographical address he gave off-the-cuff at a dinner held in his honor. Also there is the most exhaustive bibliography of his books, review, and articles to be found anywhere.

Perhaps one final note is due in regard to the relation between Latourette and what we have called the issue of the infra-structure of Christianity. Latourette was brought up in a denomination that rejected the connectional concept of church government. This in itself may have given him special sympathy for any kind of non-churchly Christian organization which he encountered in his historical researches. But then also he was mightily influenced by the non-churchly Student Volunteer Movement. He went out to China under the non-churchly Yale-In-China mission. He later worked for the independent institution, Yale University, never took the standard course for ecclesiastical ordination, though he was ordained a Baptist minister. He worked closely with the non-churchly YMCA, and dozens of other such organizations, and followed John R. Mott and his many friends in such highly mobile activities.

None of his books merely studies Churches, but all of them encompass the infra-structure of the Christian move-

A History of the Expansion of Christianity (7 Volumes)

Christianity in a Revolutionary Age (5 Volumes)

A COMPARISON OF LATOURETTE'S TWO MAJOR WORKS

Figure 10

Vol. I	AD 1-500	THE FIRST FIVE CENTURIES
Vol. II	500-1500	A THOUSAND YEARS OF UNCERTAINTY
Vol. III	1500-1815	THREE CENTURIES OF ADVANCE
Vol. IV	1815-1914	THE GREAT CENTURY: EUROPE AND THE USA
Vol. V	1815-1914	THE GREAT CENTURY: THE AMERICAS, AUSTRAL-ASIA, AFRICA
Vol. VI	1815-1914	THE GREAT CENTURY: NORTHERN AFRICA, AND ASIA
Vol. VII	1914-1944	ADVANCE THROUGH STORM

Vol. I — 19th CENTURY IN EUROPE BACKGROUND AND ROMAN CATHOLIC PHASE

Vol. II — 19th CENTURY IN EUROPE PROTESTANT AND EASTERN CHURCHES

Vol. III — 19th CENTURY OUTSIDE EUROPE AMERICAS, PACIFIC, ASIA, AFRICA

Vol. IV — 20th CENTURY IN EUROPE ROMAN CATHOLIC, PROTESTANT AND EASTERN CHURCHES

Vol. V — 20th CENTURY OUTSIDE EUROPE

EUROPE IN THE 19th CENTURY — 954 pp / 59pp

USA IN THE 19th CENTURY — 246 pp / 293 pp

NON-WESTERN WORLD IN THE 19th CENTURY — 243 pp / 926 pp

EUROPE IN THE 20th CENTURY — 238 pp

USA IN THE 20th CENTURY — 132 pp / 56pp

LATIN AMERICA IN THE 20th CENTURY — 83 pp / 35pp / 21

NON-WESTERN WORLD IN THE 20th CENTURY. — 319 pp / 350pp

ment. He was not exactly the Apostle of Christian infrastructure, but was, no doubt unintentionally, very close to this. He was always loyal to the church structures, but never supposed that God did not rely on other structures as well. It seems likely that he would have been in agreement with the thrust of the following article.

C

The Anatomy
of the Christian Mission

RALPH D. WINTER

I f it be true that second century Christians sometimes formed themselves into burial clubs in order to achieve a type of organization legal under Roman law, then that fact could give the Czechs, the Basques, and other oppressed minorities today some good ideas on how to run an underground church in an unconventional form. The whole matter of unconventional forms of the church reminds one of the incident when Charlie Brown asked Lucy what church she belonged to, and she replied that she didn't belong to a church but to a coffee house.

The amazing thing looking back over the centuries is that the essential ingredients of Christian worship and fellowship have taken on or taken over so many different kinds of structures. The Jesuits and the Salvation Army operate a structure drawn in part from a military pattern. Some indigenous Pentecostal churches overseas have grown up so isolated from historic ecclesiastical structures that they have adapted for their needs what is apparently a business structure, and it works with startling efficiency. On the other hand, it isn't any secret that the Roman Church as a whole has prospered, struggled, and in an age of democracy more recently staggered under a governmental pattern borrowed in countless aspects from the civil structure of the Roman Empire. The early Quakers, the Plymouth Brethren, the restorationist Churches of Christ, and others, have been determined to go back to the structure of the "New Testament Church," which itself was obviously borrowed mainly from the synagogue. In his case, Calvin talked about the New Testament Church, but no doubt unconsciously drew a good deal of his church order from the civil government of the Swiss canton. This was probably the source of the now-rare "collegiate ministry" in the Reformed tradition, where there is no one senior pastor, but a group of equal pastors.

But elastic as the word *church* is, it is rarely stretched to fit a whole group of now-common structures such as the above mentioned coffee house, the Inter-Varsity Bible study group, the International Christian Leadership "prayer breakfast," the shipboard Navigator prayer cell, and so on. The fact that Christ is among those two or three that gather together in His Name doesn't apparently decide the issue: most ecclesiastics will generously acknowledge all these structures as part of Christendom, but not as specifically "church" structures. Thus, out go the second century burial clubs; out go the small groups. And where, pray tell, can you fit in that most curious and influential Spanish movement called Opus Dei?

Indeed, it is to some extent today the very variety and vitality of all these "non-churchly" structures that leads some of the younger turks among theologians to wonder out loud whether the traditional institution of the church is really necessary. Harvey Cox, in referring to the Inter-Varsity Christian Fellowship in *The Secular City,* speaks of "the strength and tenacity of this remarkable organization." He goes out of his way to object to IVCF's "indefensible theology," but he is impressed by its unique structural ability that allows it to live within the university world. In fact, some of these theologians even wonder if we can't get along entirely without that moss-covered, club structure that conducts mild-mannered and mainly meaningless formal religious rites at the sacred hours

Rev. Ralph D. Winter (B.S. Caltech, M.A. Columbia U., Ph.D. Cornell U., B.D. Princeton Theological Seminary) is associate professor of missions at the School of World Mission and Institute of Church Growth, Fuller Theological Seminary, Pasadena, Calif. He served two terms under the National Evangelical Presbyterian Church as a fraternal worker of the United Presbyterian Church in the U.S.A. Last year he was executive secretary of the Latin American Association of Theological Schools, Northern Region.

on Sunday morning. Where that kind of a description is accurate, the conclusion is hard to avoid. This is why to such people, immersed as they are in a veritable sea of nominality, the phrase *church renewal* is *the mission* today.

No, not quite. These same young turks would assure us that the ultimate mission is to remake society itself. In any case, note that the mission is definitely *not* to *extend* the church. These men are so fed up with nominality that more of the same is worse, not better. They would rather slim the church down before, or instead of, extending it. Thus McGavran's church growth analysis is for them precisely the wrong thing at the wrong time. And, for them and their churches it may well be, unless they discover (1) that McGavran does not merely mean numerical growth by his famous phrase, and (2) he certainly is not talking about multiplying *dead* churches.

But if neither the nature nor the mission of the church is wonderfully clear these days, what about the various explicitly "mission structures"? If we are not clear about the results desired, how can we be clear about the kinds of instruments needed? Ruben Lores has a stimulating article entitled "The Mission of Missions" in the spring, 1968, issue of the *Evangelical Missions Quarterly*. He stresses very well the need for truly international and supranational mission structures, but does not actually spell out the precise mission of missions. Replying in the summer issue, C. Peter Wagner points out the need to distinguish between "church-related" missions and "service-related" missions, suggesting that the latter are more readily internationalized than the former. Does the structure of a mission affect its purpose and vice-versa?

It is in fact the very purpose of this article to emphasize that further conversation about the mission of missions must be based upon a clear idea of what the fundamental structures of mission are. As an attempt to stir up more thinking on this subject, I would like to propose as a tentative vocabulary of discussion the use of two terms: *vertical structures* and *horizontal structures*. The two words *vertical* and *horizontal* come from current discussion of the labor movement. The strife between the AFL and the CIO was in great part due to the fact that the AFL consisted primarily of craft unions which, for example, took in all the carpenters across the United States, no matter what company employed them, whereas the CIO felt it was better to organize all the workers of a single industry, whatever their craft. The craft unions running horizontally across the whole country, specializing in a single purpose, were thus *horizontal* unions. The industry-wide unions, like the United Auto Workers, which took in all the workers in a given automobile company, running vertically from the man who swept the floors clear up to the shop foreman, were in turn called *vertical* unions. With such very different approaches to organization, it is easy to see why the AFL and CIO broke apart and stayed apart for so long. The carpenter working for an automobile company was being wooed by both the carpenters union of the AFL and the auto workers union of the CIO. Both unions are after the same dues.

One immediately can see the parallels here between the AFL-CIO on the one hand and the IFMA-EFMA on the other hand. The mission agencies of the IFMA (the *Interdenominational* Foreign Mission Association) run horizontally across the whole country, and even to other countries, expressing the concerns of a mission-minded minority within many different Christian denominations. The EFMA (Evangelical Foreign Missions Association) on the other hand, mainly contains mission agencies that express the mission interest of whole denominations (though of course EFMA includes some horizontal agencies as well, as we shall see below.) One would not be surprised if some of the impediments to greater collaboration between EFMA and IFMA derive at least in part from the structural differences between the horizontal and vertical agencies. Indeed, the marvel is that so much good will and collaboration already exits. Not only is the horizontal a very different kind of an organization, but ultimately is competing for the same dollar of the person within a denomination that often has its own denominational mission. This is a recipe for tension.

Let us go on to make the further distinction between the internal, home-support structure of a mission agency and the structure of the results it is trying to accomplish on the field. For example, the Board of Foreign Missions of the Christian Reformed Church is the major agency expressing the foreign mission interest of that particular Christian "family." This agency, according to our definition, is a *vertical* structure at home. It goes overseas to Nigeria and among other things sets up a similar *vertical* communion—*e.g.*, a church denomination. In this sense it is a *vertical-vertical* mission because its internal home support structure is *vertical*, and its field results are *vertical*. This is represented symbolically in Diagram A.

INTERNAL
Home Support Structure

EXTERNAL
Field Results Structure

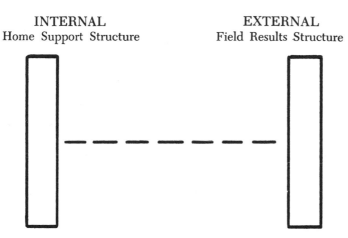

Diagram A: Foreign Board of Missions of the Christian Reformed Church, or Assemblies of God, or Southern Baptist Convention, etc.

On the other hand, the Andes Evangelical Mission is *horizontal-vertical*. In its support structure it reaches horizontally across a number of denominations and countries, but then in its Andean mission field in Bolivia (and now Peru) the primary focus of its attention is that of a single denomination, though it does have a limited interdenominational outreach. It is working in each of these two countries with what are presently the largest Protestant denominations—namely vertical structures. Along with other internally horizontal missions, it has helped create these national churches. It is thus horizontal in internal or home-support structure, but almost entirely vertical in its field results. (See Diagram B.) On the other hand, the Latin America Mission, which has a horizontal support structure, just as does the Andes Evangelical Mission, is almost entirely horizontal in its work, and only as a minor phase of its work in Costa Rica and Colombia does it focus its work on a single vertical result. Thus compare Diagram C with B.

INTERNAL
Home Support Structure

EXTERNAL
Field Results Structure

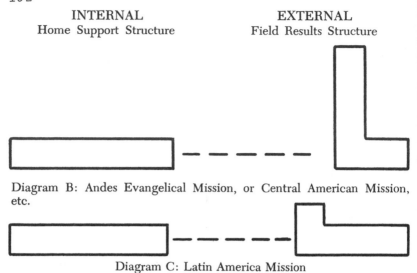

Diagram B: Andes Evangelical Mission, or Central American Mission, etc.

Diagram C: Latin America Mission

Of course, in regard to field results, what we here call horizontal missions are what many people have all along called "service missions" or "functional missions." Many of such missions are horizontal also in their support structure. Take the American Bible Society or the Missionary Aviation Fellowship, for example. They are *horizontal-horizontal* missions. Their money and people come *from* many denominations, and their activities on the field are services *to* many denominations.

Diagram D: American Bible Society, Missionary Aviation Fellowship, etc.

(See Diagram D.) It is really very logical that if the results of a mission are a specific technical service of interest to many different churches, that it be supported by many different denominations in the first place. What is not so likely is the case where a mission would operate horizontally on the field, doing a specific service for many different churches, and yet have a vertical support structure back home.

An example of a mission that is at least in part *vertical-horizontal* would thus be the one that operates the Spanish language school in Costa Rica, through which three-fourths of all the missionaries in Latin America have come. This school is the agency of a single U.S. denomination (the United Presbyterian), though it is a valuable service to over fifty other missions. The same church also sponsors other horizontal services, such as schools of all kinds (ranging from missionary children's schools to technical vocational institutes) which in most cases are clearly intended to be of service to more than Presbyterians. The same is true of some other denominational missions. However, despite the fact that the United Presbyterians operate in a vertical-horizontal way in all these specific programs, the bulk of their work is at least mostly vertical-vertical. (See Diagram E.) Why? Because their internal, home

INTERNAL
Home Support Structure

EXTERNAL
Field Results Structure

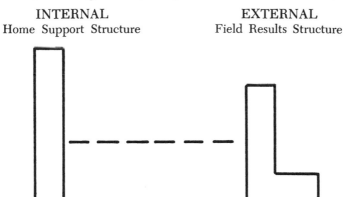

Diagram E: United Presbyterian overseas missions

support structure is a single North American denomination (a vertical structure), and their external, field results are mainly national churches, which in our terminology are similarly vertical. Even those missions mentioned in Diagram A will have, no doubt, at least some activity that serves other denominations (e.g., the Southern Baptists have their excellent publication house, Casa Bautista) so the difference between Diagrams A and E is of course a matter of degree, not kind.

The structural profile may become slightly more complex when you diagram a whole association of missions. Whereas the IFMA as a whole (See Diagram F) looks very much like something halfway between Diagrams B and C, the EFMA membership includes both missions with horizontal home structures and missions with vertical home structures, as in Diagram G. Some people would thus characterize the EFMA as more "churchly" than the IFMA, since many of its member missions are related officially to denominations as such.

INTERNAL
Home Support Structure

EXTERNAL
Field Results Structure

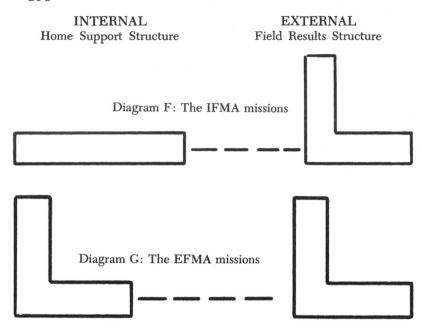

Diagram F: The IFMA missions

Diagram G: The EFMA missions

The support structures behind missionaries under five different groupings can be compared in the same way. As yet no effective study has been made of how many missionaries are in vertical or horizontal work on the field. But if we limit ourselves to indicating solely the number involved in the two different kinds of support structures back home, it is not too difficult to categorize them by whole agencies as either denominational or interdenominational, that is, vertical or horizontal. In Diagram H, then, you note that the number of missionaries sent out by denominational missions in the Division of Overseas Ministries (of the National Council of Churches in the U.S.A.) is 97 percent of the DOM total, since the DOM membership and affiliated boards include denominational sending agencies.[1] At the other extreme is the IFMA, where 100 percent of the missionaries are sent out by horizontal agencies. Note that the width of the bars in Diagram H indicates the total number of missionaries.

It is obvious that the major *polarization* here is between the DOM and the IFMA, and that the major structural *combination* is the EFMA. (The unaffiliated missions are about half and half, but are not an association.) The present collaboration between the EFMA and the IFMA is thus very signifi-

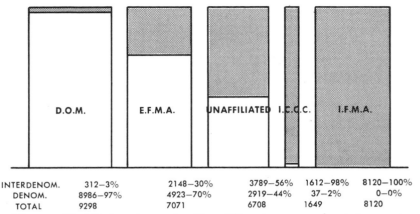

INTERDENOM.	312–3%	2148–30%	3789–56%	1612–98%	8120–100%
DENOM.	8986–97%	4923–70%	2919–44%	37–2%	0–0%
TOTAL	9298	7071	6708	1649	8120

Diagram H: Missionaries under five different groups of missions, categorized according to the internal, home support structure of their mission. TOTAL INTERDENOMINATIONAL, 15,981; DENOMINATIONAL, 16,865.

cant. There is, in this sense, no doubt that the joint IFMA and EFMA Committee on Cooperation and Comity has the most significant task of any group its size in modern missions today.

The reason to attach such significance to the potential relationship between the horizontal and vertical structures is greatly emphasized by a bit of reflection on the way the present situation came into being. One cannot fail to notice in any review of the history of Christian missions that the Roman Catholic tradition has for the most part harmoniously combined both vertical and horizontal structures in a dynamic balance. As we have mentioned, its overall structure is vertical since it functions as the spiritual government of a community that runs from the cradle to the grave. This structure includes the whole series of different levels, moving up from the parish priest to the diocesan bishop and then in a gigantic jump to the pope himself. It is a fact that the diocese of the Roman Church was originally identical in boundaries to a civil district of the same name in the Roman Empire. Similarly, the College of Cardinals corresponds to the old Roman Senate. This is only one of many indications that the overall structure of the Roman Church is an adaptation of civil or municipal government to the orderly structuring of the Christian community.

[1]It would be equally possible to make a similar chart based on the number of *agencies* or the amount of *money* (instead of *missionaries*). However, it would seem that the number of missionaries is the most illuminating single measure. The general proportions are all we desire at this point. The data themselves come from the 1965 IFMA report. It is to be noted that there is an overlap of some 600 missionaries who are under missions which belong to both the EFMA and the IFMA.

However, very early in Christian history there emerged a quite different structure of overarching importance to the history of missions: the Catholic orders. Unlike the diocesan structure, which was patterned after and complimented by the existing civil structure, the Catholic orders were a complete reconstitution of human society. They were a totally separate way of life. The famous Benedictine rule (or *regula*, from which comes *regular* priest) was in effect the new constitution of a new society which was at once separate from, and yet at least tenuously subject to, the diocesan structure. It is said that five hundred other orders have drawn on the Benedictine rule in forming their own. When Luther joined the Augustinians, he passed from the secular world into a separate "religious" world. He became thus a "religious" or "regular" priest, rather than a "secular" priest. We still speak of the Army "regulars" who have a long-term vow.

We cannot take time to describe even some of the clashes between these two types of structures, such as the conflict between the Franciscans and the bishops in the Philippines, which was fairly recent, speaking historically. For Protestants the matter of awesome significance is that Luther not only rejected the Roman church but specifically the Augustinian order, and with it the very concept of an order. That is, he not only rejected Roman control over the German diocesan structure, but he entirely abolished the horizontal structures themselves (*e.g.*, the celibate orders) of the Roman tradition. Reflecting as he did the distinctive attitudes of the Teutonic cultural substratum, he spurned determinedly the vows of celibacy, but perhaps unthinkingly eliminated their structural vehicle, which at first glance must have seemed to him inoperable apart from celibacy. Perhaps he threw the baby out with the bath.

This in turn sheds light on something with which Protestant scholars have wrestled anxiously: the near-total absence of Christian missions in the Protestant tradition throughout the first three hundred years following the Reformation. Scholars have devised many explanations, quoting the reasons or the lack of reasoning of the reformers themselves. But surely one monumental factor is simply the total absence of the structural vehicle of missions.

Confirming this hypothesis is the fact that when Protestant missions did finally appear, they appeared without exception as horizontal structures and not as the enterprises of official church or denominational boards. Dozens of horizontal mission societies burst into existence before any denomination as such set up its own official mission board. Furthermore, when such denominational boards did appear, the structure of the situation was not really what we have today. In Europe, according to one analysis, there were state churches and sects, while in the United States there was no state church and (therefore) there were no sects. These early denominations were something new under the sun.

Indeed American church historians point out that many U.S. denominations in their early existence were very much like orders, and thus quite capable of focusing officially on specific mission exploits. The present Presbyterian synod of Pittsburgh derives in part from what in 1802 had a complete synod structure, but refused to call itself a church, going rather by the name *The Western Mission Society*. When that frontier mission society constituted itself into a second coterminous organization called the *Western Foreign Mission Society*, the situation was not so much that of a "church" expressing itself in mission as it was the case of an elite Protestant "order" expressing itself in mission. The comparable Methodist work on the frontier involved circuit riders who, according to Latourette, effectively operated under the same vows of poverty, chastity and obedience which we commonly associate with the Catholic orders. Such Protestant "orders" in those days, though they were indeed emergent denominations, were by no means the nominal, internally diversified, conglomerate, "respectable" churches of today in which over half of secular society has membership. They were, in fact, an embattled, even fanatical minority, a network of highly committed individuals who dragged their first-generation families with them. The major difference between these emergent denominations and the Catholic orders was that they allowed marriage: this is probably the chief factor in the inevitable transition from eliteness to nominality. Whereas the Roman orders ostensibly recruit only members of mature choice, the Protestant denominations have absorbed the children of their members with the inevitable tendency to give those children the benefit of the doubt. (Jonathan Edwards was removed from his pulpit as the result of his attempt to stave off this irresistible process.)

This curious, "community-wide nepotism" within the church is not readily avoided. Apparently no group of committed families has ever been able to guarantee the purity and early passion of their movement by depending in any great part upon biological continuity. Indeed, where there is a fall-off of constant fresh accessions of new members converted as adults, the rate of dilution of a movement's original commitment may tend to speed up. Of course, not just "dilution" takes place over the generations, but a healthy broadening. Latitude and benefit-of-doubt to new members is not entirely bad. But the whole matter of an elite horizontal structure eventually "tipping to vertical" is too involved to discuss further here, aside from noting that this process may account for part of the common suspicion of vertical structures by the proponents of horizontal structures.

There is a corresponding suspicion of horizontal structures on the part of vertical leadership. The voluntary societies have often run off with the glory. They are where the action is. Their vivid, dramatic fund-raising threatens vertical support. In part due to their late appearance, they have been labeled *human organizations* as opposed to the *divine organism* of the (vertical) church. What historians call the "resurgence of the churchly tradition" occurred during the first half of the last century in the United States and ceaselessly contrasted the voluntary societies with the true, permanent "ecclesiastical" governments which they defined as the church.

Then, too, voluntary societies that are interdenominational (as contrasted to intradenominational societies)[2] will always elicit the suspicions of those who place high value on denominational distinctives. The widely-lamented fissiparous tendency in Protestantism is in part a logical development from the fundamental Lutheran proposition that you did not need to be Roman to be Christian, for it has allowed a wide variety of nations, tribes, tongues, and peoples and subcultures and cultural strata to have their own churches. It has in effect sanctioned the diversity of vertical structures. But in so doing,

---

[2]When the Conservative Baptist Foreign Mission Society worked exclusively within the American Baptist Convention it was then an intradenominational society; now of course it is *inter*denominational, even though it is mainly still *intra*—since its support for the most part comes from the churches in the Conservative Baptist Association. In any case, the intradenominational *society* must be distinguished from the denominational mission *board*—the latter is characteristically dependent upon denominational control and budgetary support.

it has put horizontal structures in the bad light of down-playing those precious distinctives in their attempt to combine people from different home denominations in the same overseas mission.

However, we are driven back to the reformers' rejection of the horizontal structures. Even the Catholic tradition has had its problems with them, dissolving the Jesuits as it did at one crucial point. Perhaps Protestantism has been chary of the order-structure precisely because Protestantism has lacked the central authority to hold it in harness. Perhaps we need greater powers of review and evaluation on the part of the vertical structures. If the horizontal structures would more widely submit to the review of the vertical, perhaps greater confidence and collaboration could be built up. In secular society, private enterprise must submit to the review of the civil government. The Food and Drug Administration watchdogs follow carefully the food processors and the pharmaceutical houses, but they do not otherwise control them. The socialist would let the vertical civil structure control everything. The opposite extreme would be the chaos of unmonitored private firms.

In any case, structurally speaking, perhaps the most significant Protestant schism was not the disconnection of the German and Scandinavian churches from Rome, but rather was that most drastic and seemingly permanent rift between the horizontal and vertical structures. The reaffiliation of merely the Protestant *vertical* structures, in either the NAE, the NCC, or the WCC is apparently a relatively simple accomplishment by comparison, however marvelous it may seem after embarrassing centuries of division between the geographical and culturally distinct Christian communions within the Protestant tradition. But it may be a more profound and unnoticed problem that the emergence of horizontal structures in Protestantism has not yet by any means resulted in the desired unity or harmony between the separate worlds of these two disparate structures.

The solution for this kind of Protestant schism can only come about through a better understanding of the unique function, the advantages and disadvantages of each of these two kinds of structures. Hardly anyone will dispute the fact that it is better for a single horizontal agency, separate from, but dependent upon, all the denominations, to concentrate upon the specific task and the accompanying technical problems attendant upon the translation and distribution of the Bible. Thus the American Bible Society is one of the oldest and most durable of the horizontal structures and makes a notable contribution to foreign missions. It may be equally logical and impelling that a single horizontal agency like MAF should provide air service for all missions operating in many roadless areas of the world. Yet this newer organization, which has a much more technical and perhaps less "essential" ministry, is not as likely to receive an allocation of funds directly from denominational mission budgets as is the case with the American Bible Society. Would it be better if these agencies were operated under the jurisdiction of the NAE, the NCC, or the WCC? (This is in some ways like asking the question whether the post office or the telephone system should be run as part of the private or the public sphere; and if public, then should it be under U.S. federal or U.N. control?) But the technical factors of political science and sociology in such questions are not entirely understood in the secular world much less in the ecclesiastical world.

Many questions arise. Should the founding of a new church in a given country ideally be the job of a foreign church or a horizontal-vertical mission like the Overseas Missionary Fellowship, which is both international and interecclesiastical?

Another question is whether the final result of missions is merely a healthy national church without any infrastructure of horizontal organizations in that "mission land." That is, should we consider the mission task done when we have set up a viable denomination? Or, in the interest of the effective proclamation of the Gospel, do we need to make sure that not only in the U.S. but also in the mission lands there are nationally-run, semi-autonomous, horizontal mission structures that will act as the shock troops of both home and foreign missions based in that country? Precisely this is found in the Solomon Islands, where for example, the Anglican Church is greatly aided by the effective home-mission outreach of the Melanesian Brotherhood, which is an intradenominational horizontal structure working with it in harmonious semi-autonomy.[3]

[3]Describing the contribution of this structure to a significant change of pace in church growth in the Solomon Islands, Dr. Alan Tippett says, "The most important innovation in this second half-century was probably the establishment of the Melanesian Brotherhood, which made the evangelistic thrust a thoroughly indigenous mechanism, and something quite unique in Pacific Missions" (*Solomon Islands Christianity, A Study in Growth and Obstruction*, Friendship Press, 1967).

Further discussion and mature reflection upon these structural factors may give us greater insight into the situation into which God has led us. Is it desirable that vertical structures tend to give people the benefit of the doubt and that other structures involve an additional voluntary step into a more active involvement in mission? Even granting that we acknowledge a need for both the cradle-to-grave structure and also the elite structure, it may well be true that because these two types of organization are so different, they will always have to make a special effort to understand each other.

The vertical structure has greater internal diversity and may thus tend to have greater objectivity and overall perspective, but less mobility. It may tend to bureaucracy due to the "distance" between the donor and the final function. It may tend to be a caretaker structure that, again due to great internal diversity, finds it difficult to gain broad support for anything, especially enterprises beyond its immediate internal needs. The church as church finds it difficult to become excited about the spiritual fate of the urban masses in Calcutta.

The horizontal structure tends to have a more specific objective and the direct support of those behind it. It has greater potential mobility and efficiency. But it typically sees only its own goals and therefore needs overall perspective. Citizens of the Kingdom may even need protection against its capacity to oversell its cause. Yet it offers a healthy escape valve for the differing visions of the diverse elements of a heterogeneous church.

Both kinds of structures have the capacity to help or harm each other. Horizontal agencies like the Student Volunteer Movement, Christian Endeavor, Inter-Varsity, and so on, have contributed mightily to the vertical structures, and vice-versa. On the other hand, Henry Van Dusen has accused denominational leaders of moving in on college campuses and dismantling the svm. Others have watched helplessly while denominational leaders deliberately fought and severely damaged Christian Endeavor. Despite the Protestant bias against the horizontal, John Mackay has had the audacity to honor the Latin America Mission by calling it a "Protestant order." Perhaps he is especially happy about the lam's Evangelism-in-Depth program, which is history's first "master service mission," since the year-long "treatment" offered a country by eid boldly coordinates not only all vertical but all horizontal structures in a harmonious matrix of a fabulous potential, which precisely surmounts the Protestant schism.

In this brief presentation many details have had to be left out, and many others remain unresolved. One thing seems clear: the fact that in Protestant missions many of the most significant forward steps in both the strategy of support, and the strategy of overseas operations, depend upon a far better understanding than we now have of the "anatomy of the Christian mission."

(Reprinted by permission of the Evangelical Missions Quarterly.)

Reference Notes

CHAPTER 1
1. Some will argue that the Chinese were never conquered, and in the conventional political sense, this is true. But the imposition of opium on China by the Europeans during more than a half century and the ensuing period of gunboat diplomacy represent sufficient tyranny by outsiders to satisfy our loose definition of domination. Certainly in 1951 the Chinese gained relatively greater freedom from external European domination, and with the expulsion of the Russians in the early 1960s, the European retreat was complete.
2. Sukarno, "Selected Documents of the Bandung Conference," (Asia-African Conference at Bandung, Indonesia, April 18-24, 1955) p. 4. A mimeographed paper available from the Institute of Pacific Relations, New York.

CHAPTER 2
3. Van Dusen, Henry Pitney, *They Found the Church There*, N.Y.: Scribners, 1945.
4. Latourette, Kenneth Scott, *Christianity Through the Ages*, N.Y.: Harper and Row, 1965, p. 299.
5. Tippett, A. R., *Verdict Theology in Missionary Theory*, Lincoln, Illinois: Lincoln Christian College Press, 1969, p. 129.
6. McGavran, Donald, *Understanding Church Growth*, New York: Oxford, 1968, p.299.
7. Cragg, Kenneth, *Christianity in World Perspective*, N.Y.:Oxford, 1968, pp. 13,14.
8. Barrett, David, *Schism and Renewal in Africa: An Analysis of 6,000 Contemporary Religious Movements*, Nairobi: Oxford, 1968.
9. Sundkler, B.G.M., *Bantu Prophets in South Africa*, 2nd. ed., London: Oxford, 1961.
10. Swanson, Allan, "A Comparative Study of Independent and Mainline Churches in Taiwan," a master's thesis presented June, 1968 and available from the School of World Mission, Fuller Theological Seminary, Pasadena, Calif.
11. Read, Monterroso, and Johnson, *Church Growth in Latin America*, Grand Rapids: Eerdmans, p. 252.
12. Allen, Roland, *Missionary Methods: St. Paul's or Ours*, London: World Dominion Press, 1930. Also *The Spontaneous Expansion of the Church and the Causes Which Hinder It*, London: World Dominion Press, 1927.
13. *World Vision Magazine*, Monrovia, Calif.
14. Anderson, Gerald H., ed., *The Theology of the Christian Mission*, N.Y.: McGraw Hill Book Company, 1965, paperback edition, p. 111.
15. Rian, Edwin H., ed., *Christianity and World Revolution*, N.Y.: Harper and Row, 1963, pp. 149-150.
16. *Church Growth Bulletin*, Palo Alto, Calif., or School of World Mission, Fuller Theological Seminary, Pasadena, Calif.
17. Ibid., Volume 5, No. 5, May 1969.
18. *Time*, January 12, 1970, p. 35.
19. Read, Monterroso and Johnson, Op. Cit., p. 58.
20. Schonfield, Hugh J., *Those Incredible Christians*, N.Y.: Bantam Books, 1968.
21. Latourette, Kenneth Scott, *The Christian Mission in Our Day*, N.Y.: Harper and Brothers, 1954, p. 80.
22. Latourette, Kenneth Scott, *A History of Christianity*, N.Y.: Harper and Row, 1954, p. 941.
23. Swanson, Op. Cit.
24. Dewart, Leslie, "Have We Loved the Past Too Long?" *America* 115, No. 25: pp. 798-802.
25. Henry, Carl F.H., "The Reality and Identity of God," *Christianity Today* 13, No. 13, March 28, 1969, p. 594.
26. Masatoshi Doi, "Introduction to a Theology of Mission," *Studies in the Christian Religion* (Kirisutokyo Kenku), Vol. 33, No. 4: pp. 1-5. Published by the School of Theology, Doshisha University, Kyoto, Japan.
27. Dr. Donald R. Jacobs, Box 7596, Nairobi, Kenya, East Africa.
28. Latourette, Kenneth Scott, *Challenge and Conformity*, N.Y.: Harper and Brothers, 1955, pp. 20-23.
29. Barrett, Op. Cit., p. 130.
30. Beaver, R. Pierce, *From Missions to Mission*, N.Y.: Association Press Reflection Book, 1964, p. 103.
31. Ibid., p. 61.

CHAPTER 3
32. Cragg, Op. Cit., p. 210.
33. Latourette, Kenneth Scott, *Christianity in a Revolutionary Age, Vol. 5,*
    N.Y.: Harper and Row, 1962, p. 526.
34. Ibid., Vol. 4, p. 521.
35. Ibid., Vol. 1, p. ix of Preface.
36. Cragg, Op. Cit., p. 66.
37. Winter, Ralph D., "Church Growth Calculations, Facts and Fallacies, No. 2,"
    Church Growth Bulletin, Vol. 6, No. 5, May, 1970.
38. Barrett, David, "The Expansion of Christianity in Africa in the Twentieth
    Century," *Church Growth Bulletin,* Vol. 5, No. 5, May, 1969, pp. 362-6.
39. Beaver, Op. Cit., p. 63.
40. Read, Monterroso and Johnson, Op. Cit., p. 49.
41. Ibid., p. 268.
42. In this series of terms the wqrd *Evangelical* refers to those whose faith
    could be traced to the characteristic emphasis of the Evangelical Awakening
    on a decisive personal experience with Christ and a resulting assurance of
    salvation.
43. Degnan, James P., "The Nonsense of Liberal Catholics," *Christianity Today,*
    Nov. 21, 1969, pp. 3-6.
44. Van Leeuwen, Arend Th., *Christianity in World History,* N.Y.: Charles Scribner's
    Sons, 1964, pp. 331-4, 375, 402, 410, 417.
45. Mackay, John, *Christian Reality and Appearance,* Richmond: John Knox Press,
    1969, p. 88.
CHAPTER 4
46. Hogg, William Richie, *Ecumenical Foundations: A History of the International
    Missionary Council and Its Nineteenth-Century Background.* New York: Harper
    and Brothers, 1952, p. 307. Also see *The World Christian Community in
    Action: The Story of World War II and the Orphaned Missions* by Latourette
    and Hogg, New York: The International Missionary Council, 1949.
47. Horner, Norman A., ed., *Protestant Crosscurrents in Missions,* N.Y.: Abing-
    don, 1968, p. 39.
48. Goodall, Norman, ed., *Missions Under the Cross,* London: Morrison and Gibb,
    Limited, 1953, p. 40.
49. Latourette, Kenneth Scott, *Missions Tomorrow,* N.Y.: Harper and Brothers,
    1936, pp. 127-31.
50. Latourette, Kenneth Scott and William Richie Hogg, *Tomorrow is Here,* N.Y.:
    Friendship Press, 1948.
51. Stowe, David,"Changing Patterns of Missionary Service in Today's World,"
    Occasional Bulletin, Vol. XX, No. 1, January 1969, (N.Y. Missionary Research Lib
52. Beaver, Op. Cit., p. 73.
53. Latourette, *Christianity in a Revolutionary Age, Vol. 5,* Op. Cit. pp. 4, 15;
    also *The Emergence of a World Christian Community,* New Haven: Yale University
    Press, 1949, pp. 10, 11, 60, 61, 74-5, 83.
54. Van Leeuwen, Op. Cit., chapter eight.
55. Bradshaw, Malcolm R., *Church Growth Through Evangelism-in-Depth,* So. Pasadena,
    Calif.: William Carey Library, 1969.
56. Beaver, Op. Cit.
57. Ibid., p. 81.
58. Mackay, John, "The Ecumenical Tomorrow," *World Vision Magazine,* April, 1970,
    p. 5.
59. Latourette, *A History of Christianity,* Op. Cit., pp. 1344-45.
60. Latourette, *A History of the Expansion of Christianity, Vol. 7,* N.Y.: Harper
    and Brothers, 1944, p. 29.
61. Winter, Ralph D., "The Anatomy of the Christian Mission," *Evangelical Missions
    Quarterly,* Vol. 5, No. 2, Winter, 1969, p. 74. See pages 97-116 this book.
62. Hogg, Op, Cit., p. 9.
CHAPTER 5
63. Bradshaw, Op. Cit.
64. Winter, Ralph D., ed., *Theological Education by Extension,* South Pasadena:
    William Carey Library, 1969.
65. Beaver, Op. Cit., pp. 104-5.
66. News Item, "Coming Soon: An Ecumenical Overhaul," *Christianity Today,* Feb.
    13, 1970, pp. 44-6.

67. The William Carey Library established in 1969 in South Pasadena, California is an example of a publishing house which serves a specialized market, in this case those interested in missions.

68. The school mentioned is the School of World Missions and Institute
68. of Church Growth at Fuller Theological Seminary in Pasadena, California.

69. MARC is a subsidiary of World Vision, Monrovia, California.

70. Daystar Communications, Inc., 1432 Orchard Street, Eugene, Oregon.

71. Latourette, Kenneth Scott, *Missions Tomorrow*, Op. Cit., pp. 213-15.

Epilogue

THE TASK BEFORE US

Adapted from an address at the International Congress on World Evangelization at Lausanne, Switzerland, July 20, 1974

The period of the twenty-five unbelievable years (1945-69) is now past, and we are into a new era. Many mission and church leaders around the world have stated that the job of world evangelization is mainly done, and that the remaining task can be completed by national churches. Some have even spoken of a "moratorium on missionaries." This kind of thinking is not limited to the liberal churchmen nor to the older denominations. Whole mission societies have sprung up with the concept of "national missionaries only" as their basic *raison de etre.*

Yet one wonders if anyone has really analyzed the task yet remaining. Do we know how many non-Christians there are in the world who have never been given a viable opportunity to know Christ? Do we know where these are? Where millions have seemed resistant to the gospel, has anyone studied why? Is the national church around the world even physically able to complete the task of world evangelization? These are serious questions which have waited too long for answers. What does the Holy Spirit say to us today? Does the Great Commission still apply, and to whom?

Here in this epilogue we have space only to consider the scope of the task remaining in world evangelization. Jesus said that no man builds a tower without first sitting down and calculating the cost. Figure 1 is an attempt to do that. For simplification I have divided the world into three major blocs: the Western world, Africa, and Asia. Australia and Latin America are included in the Western world; the Pacific I have placed in the column titled Asia.

CHRISTIANS	Western	Africa	Asia	TOTAL	
Nurture	120	40	40	200	
E-0 Renewal	845	76	58	979	
	965	116	98	1179	
NON-CHRISTIANS					
E-1 Ord. Ev.	180	82	74	336	------13%
E-2,E-3, CC Ev.	147	200	2040	2387	------87%
	327	282	2114	2723	
GRAND TOTAL	1292	398	2212	3902	

FIGURE 1

Note also that the numbers in the chart are all in <u>millions</u> of people in the world today. You will see I have first divided between those who call themselves Christians and those who do not call themselves Christians, and you will see in the column on the far right that the total number of Christians is 1179 million, and the total number of non-Christians is 2723 million. These two numbers, 1179 and 2723 are, of course, not precise counts except at a certain date; they are only apparently static. They do not show, for example, the fact that the percentage of Christians is constantly gaining in all columns—that is, in the Western World, Africa and Asia.

Now note that both the Christian and the non-Christian populations have been further divided on our chart. The Christian group is divided into 1) the committed Christians, who need nurture, and 2) the nominal Christians, who need renewal. The non-Christians are also divided in two groups: 1) those who can be reached by ordinary, near-neighbor evangelism (which I have called E-1 evangelism), and 2) those who are beyond a significant cultural frontier, <u>whom we can only reach by cross cultural evangelism</u>. (This type of evangelism I have called E-2 or E-3 evangelism.) In a word, these are people at a sufficient cultural distance so that we cannot necessarily expect them to join existing Christian churches, and they may wish to exercise their Biblical right to self-determination in establishing a separate cultural tradition of regular worship

and fellowship. Their existences calls for special cross-cultural evangelism, and constitutes what I believe is the major
technical obstacle to world evangelization today.

In Figure 2 you see the quantities and distinctions mentioned in Figure 1 now visualized with the spaces drawn to
scale. For example, the four numbers down the right side of
the larger, vertical rectangle -- 200, 979, 336, 2387 -- are
the same numbers we have just seen in the last column of Figure
1. The first two numbers are those who call themselves Christians, requiring nurture and renewal. Then you'll notice a
dark line running across the rectangle, and the two categories
below this line are the non-Christians -- the 336 million who
can be reached by the ordinary evangelism of Christians reaching out to their cultural near-neighbors, and 2387 million who
are not within the range of the ordinary evangelism of any
Christian congregation, that is, people who require cross-cultural evangelism (E-2 or E-3). Note that according to these
estimates, 87% of the non-Christians are in the cross-cultural
category. Before leaving this diagram, note that most of the
people needing renewal are in the Western World, while the
people needing cross-cultural evangelism are mainly in Asia.
This is not surprising since the gospel came first to the Western World, and after generations the children and grandchil-
dren of committed Christians still call themselves Christians,
but may never attend church or pray. Asia, on the other hand,
is so vast that what evangelism has been done there in the past
is still like a drop in the bucket of her multitudes. This difference between the types of people to be evangelized in Asia
and the West helps to account for the instinctive difference
between the way most Western Christians think about evangelism
and the way people involved in cross-cultural work think about
evangelism.

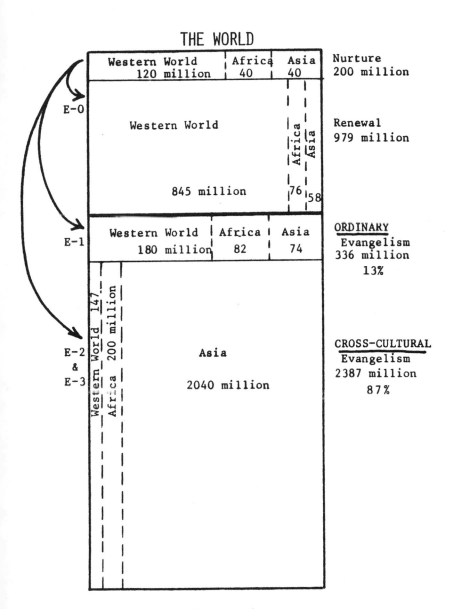

FIGURE 2

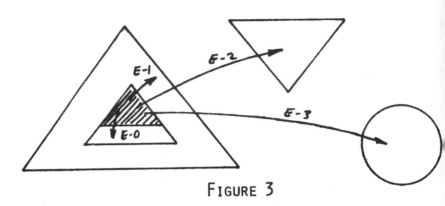

FIGURE 3

Now let's look at Figure 3. Here you see a small triangl
representing the Christian community, from which four arrows
emerge. One arrow, labelled E-0, is aimed into a sector withi
the Christian community. This is the winning of nominal Chris
tians to personal faith and commitment -- the "evangelical experience." This E-0 evangelism involves just as much a spirit
ual experience as E-1, E-2, or E-3 evangelism, but there is no
cultural barrier to be crossed -- hence the zero. That is,
these people are not only from the same secular culture, they
have also had contact with the church to some extent. The arrow labelled E-1 goes out of the church into the culture withi
which the church is at home, the only barrier here being the
"stained-glass barrier" between the church and the world.
People in this E-1 area, if converted, will feel at home in
existing churches.

The E-2 arrow, however, reaches outside the culture in
which the church finds itself and reaches into one that is si
lar but nevertheless sufficiently different to make the founding of separate congregations desirable to act as a base for
effective outreach to others in that same culture. An exampl
here might be the rock culture of U.S. youth, or a slightly
more distant culture involving a foreign language, such as th
Mexican-American culture areas of Los Angeles. In both cases
it probably would be desirable to set up separate congregatio
for new Christians won from these cultures so that they can m
easily reach out to their own people and win them to Christ a
the church. The E-3 arrow involves similar church-planting i
plications, but reaches out to a totally strange culture (the
circle). An example of an E-3 culture in Los Angeles would b
the Navajo Indians, who number over 20,000.

I hope this doesn't seem too complicated. It is a help when looking at any country or region of the world to size up the situation by making a rough estimate of the number of people in each of these five categories which the diagram in Figure 3 gives us: First, there are the committed Christians (shaded area) who are the only active agents you can count on to do the work. Next there are the four kinds of people who are not committed Christians and who are either at a 0, 1, 2 or 3 cultural distance away from the committed Christians. Following this scheme, you can divide the people in a small town into these five categories. Or you can make estimates of the number of people in these five categories for a whole country. This seems to be helpful to size up the task.

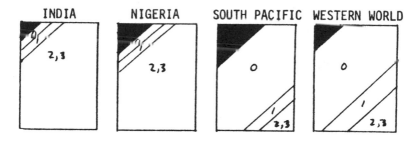

FIGURE 4

I have done this by way of example in the diagrams in Figure 4. The first three diagrams are for three different sections of the non-Western world, where from left to right there is a progressively greater number of committed Christians, represented by the shaded areas. (In these diagrams I have not distinguished between the E-2 and E-3 areas because they both involve cross-cultural evangelism and therefore usually require founding new churches.) The fourth diagram -- the Western World -- shows the close comparison between the South Pacific and the Western World. In both cases a high proportion of the people are at least nominal Christians, and this means that the need for cross-cultural evangelism internal to the regions may not seem so important to people in these areas. Clearly, their largest task is winning nominal Christians (E-0).

On the other hand, India and Nigeria are more typical of all the rest of the world, and that is why cross-cultural evangelism is of the highest priority in the non-Western world. For example, there are a lot of Christians in India, many of whom may need their faith renewed, but in terms of proportions the real task of evangelization there is in the E-2, E-3 sphere. Let me say it more bluntly: most of the people in India are at

a cross-cultural distance from any Christian congregation
whatsoever.

   In Figures 5 and 6, unlike in the table in Figure 1, we
have divided the total world populations first into Western and
non-Western spheres. In Figure 5 you'll notice the statistics
from the first column of the table in Figure 1, where the Western world is divided between Christian and non-Christian --965
million Christians and 327 million non-Christians. Note that
the 10,000 missionaries working in the Western world (mainly
Europe, North America, Latin America) are focussing almost all
of their efforts on the nominal Christian sphere (E-0) while
only a fairly small percent, according to my estimates, are
really concentrating on people who do not consider themselves
Christians (E-1, E-2 and E-3). This is not surprising because
the majority of Westerners are nominal Christians. Things are
very different in the non-Western world, as we see in Figure 6.
There for greater clarification we have divided the non-Christians into four groups -- Chinese, Muslim, Hindu and "other."
The bottom three layers represent three virtually untouched
blocs of humanity, amounting to 1933 million people.

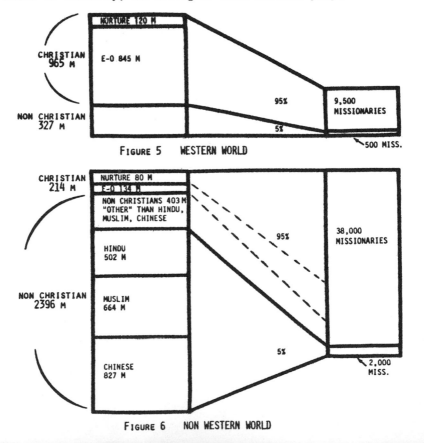

FIGURE 5   WESTERN WORLD

FIGURE 6   NON WESTERN WORLD

Let us think for a few moments about these three groups. According to Figure 1 we know that there are roughly 2723 million non-Christians in the world today. If we were to set apart only <u>one</u> cross-cultural evangelist per <u>million</u> non-Christians, in order to reach the 502 million non-Christian Hindus we would have to find 502 people whose job and calling could be focussed on these people. These would have to be cross-cultural specialists, on the whole. We would also have to have 664 people here specializing on reaching the 664 million Muslims. They too would have to be almost entirely cross-cultural specialists, since only tiny numbers of Muslims can be won by local Christians living in their areas who try to reach them by ordinary evangelism. (Parenthetically, let me observe that the Muslim group, which is already immense, is growing at a biological rate almost double that of the Chinese, and that if present rates continue, there will be more Muslims than Chinese within about ten years.) Moving on to the Chinese, proportionately to represent the 827 million non-Christian Chinese would require 827 people specializing on the task of reaching them. In the case of the Chinese there are millions of Christian Chinese to help in the task, but even so, the Chinese are so split up by dialects, social distinctions, and highly significant clan differences that most of this task is E-2 rather than E-1, and thus mainly a cross-cultural problem as with the other two major blocs.

Now note something very significant. As in the case of the Western world in Figure 5, most of the cross-cultural workers in the non-Western world (Fig. 6) are focussing their efforts on nurture and E-0 evangelism connected with the Christian community. The number of Christians both vibrant and nominal, in the non-Western world is the sum of the Africa and Asia columns in Figure 2. For Africa, these figures are 40 million + 76 million, or 116 million total, and for Asia 40 million + 58 million, or 98 million total. Together they make a grand total of 214 million Christians in Africa and Asia. Or if we merge the columns according to Christian commitment, rather than by country, we find that there are 80 million committed Christians in the non-Western world, whose nurture soaks up a very large proportion of the energies of both Christian missionaries and national church leaders; there are also 134 million nominal Christians who take up practically all of the rest of their efforts. It is only a guess, but it is safe to say that 95% of all missionaries deployed in the non-Western world are focussing their efforts either on the care and feeding of Christians, the renewal of communities that claim to be Christian, or upon non-Christian peoples in the immediate environment of the Christians, consisting mainly the 403 million

non-Christians in the "other" category in this chart.   That
leaves only a tiny percentage of cross-cultural workers to
deal with the three major blocs of non-Western non-Christians.
This is a grim picture.   The task to be done is big enough, but
precisely where the cross-cultural task is the largest, the
cross-cultural workers are the fewest.   (See Figure 6)

     For example, the number of effective evangelists winning
middle caste and upper caste Hindus (well over 400 million
people) are very few indeed.   The number of effective cross-
cultural evangelists winning Muslims is likewise small.   While
there may be proportionately more cross-cultural workers who
are reaching out to non-Christian Chinese, these would mainly
be in Taiwan.   But even in Taiwan most missionaries and nation
leaders are absorbed with the needs of the Christian community.
This is not to begrudge the "interchurch" exchange of E-3 workers.   The danger is that we may easily deceive ourselves concerning the proportionate weight of personnel that is going to
the evangelism of non-Christians.   This is so important to und
stand that we must use an extended illustration of this whole
matter of the statistical scope of the task of cross-cultural
evangelism.   Since I have already said a good deal in my origi
nal paper about Pakistan, let me build on that situation.

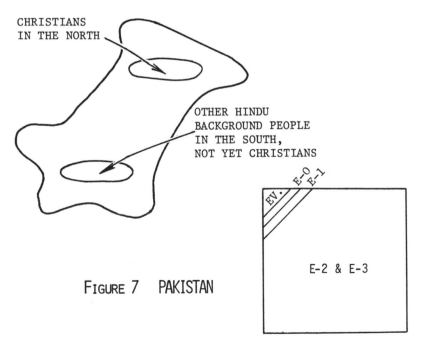

CHRISTIANS
IN THE NORTH

OTHER HINDU
BACKGROUND PEOPLE
IN THE SOUTH,
NOT YET CHRISTIANS

EV.   E-0   E-1

E-2 & E-3

FIGURE 7   PAKISTAN

The rough proportions in Pakistan are similar to the diagram in Figure 4 for India. In Pakistan there are proportionately fewer Christians than in India, but they number well over one-half million (out of 70 million). The Christian community today is the product of a great people movement and spiritual revival over a half century ago, but very few people living today were brought to Christ in that movement, and the churches of Pakistan by now have a sizeable proportion of their own members who need to be won by E-0 evangelism to personal spiritual obedience to Christ. The really surprising thing is why the E-1 sphere is so small. A country of 70 million peple where there are 500,000 Christians does not on the face of it seem likely to be a place where near-neighbor evangelism would be of relatively small significance. Why can't the 500,000 Christians just reach out to their neighbors and win them to Christ? This is a crucial question. The answer is that 99 per cent of the Christians have a Hindu (not Muslim) cultural background, whereas 97 per cent of the non-Christians in Pakistan are Muslim. In the north you have scattered communities of Christians (just as in India, most Christians are in separated, isolated areas, almost like ghettos), but their <u>physical</u> separation from so many of their countrymen does not remotely approach the significance of their <u>cultural</u> isolation.

Thus, from the beginning of the revival movement in the north over fifty years ago until the present time, almost never has a Muslim joined a Christian church, while hundreds of thousands of former Hindus have become Christians. Although the church in Pakistan has a large E-0 population of nominal Christians, it is continuing to win some remaining Hindus to Christ through E-1 evangelism. On this basis, how soon will the church run out of Hindus to convert? In the northern part of the country, where most of the Christians are, practically all of the non-Muslim people of Pakistan are already at least nominally Christian. Curiously, there are almost a million people of Hindu background yet to win, but they are in the South, hundreds of miles from the main body of Christians. While it would be relatively simple for these Christians to do evangelism in the South (only geographical distance away), the Christians are very very distant from their Muslim neighbors. Why? Because there is a very pronounced cultural distance between the cultural tradition from which the church has sprung and the cultural tradition represented by the Muslims.

Let us be more specific. Both Muslims and the (Hindu-background) Christians in the North speak Urdu. But they don't speak exactly the same kind of Urdu. A Muslim can tell either by listening or by reading that the religious language of the

Christians though Urdu, nevertheless comes from the Hindu minority community in his country, and he has monumental prejudices about this difference. The Christians, on the other hand, while they don't hate the Muslims, don't feel it is necessary to make a special translation of the New Testament into the religious language of the Urdu-speaking Muslims, even though there are more than 30 million Urdu-speaking Muslims alone! Feelings of suspicion between the two communities are so great that an occasional Muslim convert does not feel at home in any of the Christian congregations. Christians have not yet made an effective effort nor even drawn up speculative plans for the development of worshipping communities drawn wholly from the Muslim tradition. This is only natural, in a way, because the Christians come from a stratum of society which has for centuries been impoverished and virtually enslaved. The Christians even yet are barely struggling to their feet economically. Their resources, their education, their evangelistic imagination does not readily stretch to radically new ways of evangelizing the Muslims--especially not to ways that will allow the Muslims the kind of liberty in Christ which the gospel guarantees them.

What this all means is profound. It means that the three major blocs of humanity, Muslim, Hindu and Chinese, as yet unintroduced to Jesus Christ, have not at the present time a really good opportunity to understand Him. All talk about "resistant peoples" is nonsense in such a case. The ball is in our court! It is our task to utilize radically new methods and structures where necessary to do the job we have not done.

This epilogue has constituted about one-fourth of the material in the two addresses presented by Dr. Ralph D. Winter at the Lausanne Congress. The entire text, plus an introduction by Dr. Donald A. McGavran, is available as a booklet entitled The New Macedonia: A Revolutionary New Era in Missions Begins, *available post paid for 75¢ per copy or four copies for $2.00 postpaid. Order from William Carey Library, 533 Hermosa Street, South Pasadena, California 91030.*

Those who would like to read further on this subject may be interested in three other booklets by the same author: Seeing the Task Graphically, *25¢ per copy or four copies for $1.00 postpaid;* The Two Structures of God's Redemptive Mission *35¢ per copy or three copies for $1.00 postpaid;* Say Yes to Mission, *25¢ per copy or four copies $1.00 postpaid. Include 35¢ extra for postage and handling if ordering single copies of the above three booklets. Order from William Carey Library 533 Hermosa Street, South Pasadena, California 91030.*

BOOKS BY THE WILLIAM CAREY LIBRARY

GENERAL

The Birth of Missions in America by Charles L. Chaney, $7.95 paper, 352 pp.

Church Growth and Christian Mission by Donald A. McGavran, $4.95x paper, 256 pp.

Church Growth and Group Conversion by Donald A. McGavran et al., $2.45 paper, 128 pp.

Church Planting in Uganda: A Comparative Study by Gailyn Van Rheenen, $4.95 paper, 192 pp.

Crucial Dimensions in World Evangelization edited by Arthur F. Glasser et al., $6.95x paper, 480 pp.

Crucial Issues in Bangladesh by Peter McNee, $6.95 paper, 304 pp.

Education of Missionaries' Children: The Neglected Dimension of World Mission by D. Bruce Lockerbie, $1.95 paper, 76 pp.

Everything You Need to Grow a Messianic Synagogue by Phillip E. Goble, $2.45 paper, 176 pp.

Here's How: Health Education by Extension by Ronald and Edith Seaton, $3.45 paper, 144 pp.

The How and Why of Third World Missions: An Asian Case Study by Marlin L. Nelson, $6.95 paper, 256 pp.

A Manual for Church Growth Surveys by Ebbie C. Smith, $3.95 paper, 144 pp.

Protestantism in Latin America: A Bibliographical Guide edited by John H. Sinclair, $8.95x paper, 448 pp.

Reaching the Unreached by Edward C. Pentecost, $5.95 paper, 256 pp.

Readings in Third World Missions: A Collection of Essential Documents edited by Marlin L. Nelson, $6.95x paper, 304 pp.

World Handbook for the World Christian by Patrick St. J. St. G. Johnstone, $4.95 paper, 224 pp.

APPLIED ANTHROPOLOGY

Becoming Bilingual: A Guide to Language Learning by Donald Larson and William A. Smalley, $5.95x paper, 426 pp.

Christopaganism or Indigenous Christianity? edited by Tetsunao Yamamori and Charles R. Taber, $5.95 paper, 242 pp.

The Church and Cultures: Applied Anthropology for the Religious Worker by Louis J. Luzbetak, $5.95x paper, 448 pp.

Customs and Cultures: Anthropology for Christian Missions by Eugene A. Nida, $3.95x paper, 322 pp.

Manual of Articulatory Phonetics by William A. Smalley, $4.95x paper, 522 pp.

Message and Mission: The Communication of the Christian Faith by Eugene A. Nida, $3.95x, 254 pp.

Readings in Missionary Anthropology edited by William A. Smalley, $5.95x, 384 pp.

THEOLOGICAL EDUCATION BY EXTENSION

Principles of Church Growth by Wayne C. Weld and Donald A. McGavran, $4.95x paper, 400 pp.

The World Directory of Theological Education by Extension by Wayne C. Weld, $5.95x paper, 416 pp. *1976 Supplement only*, $1.95x, 64 pp.

Writing for Theological Education by Extension by Lois McKinney, $1.45x, 64 pp.

ABOUT THE AUTHOR

The Rev. Ralph D. Winter has been a Professor of the Historical Development of Christianity at the School of World Mission, Fuller Theological Seminary in Pasadena, California. His Ph.D. from Cornell University is in the field of Descriptive Linguistics and Cultural Anthropology with a minor in Mathematical Statistics. He also holds the B.S. in Engineering from the California Institute of Technology and the B.D. from Princeton Theological Seminary.

Prior to his present position, Dr. Winter served for fifteen years under the Commission on Ecumenical Mission and Relations of the United Presbyterian Church in the United States of America. Ten of those years were spent as a missionary to Guatemala where he was assigned to leadership development among Mayan Indians. He is the editor of *Theological Education by Extension*, having been one of the early pioneers of this movement which has been adapted around the world. He is the author of *The Warp and the Woof: Organizing for Mission, Seeing the Task Graphically, The Two Structures of God's Redemptive Mission*, as well as the final chapter and bibliographies updating Kenneth Scott Latourette's *A History of Christianity*. He is also the author of numerous chapters and articles in various symposia and periodicals. His condensation of *The Twenty-Five Unbelievable Years, 1945-1969* appears as the supplement to Volume VII of the Zondervan edition of Latourette's *History of the Expansion of Christianity*.

Dr. Winter is well known as a lecturer and mission strategist, and was a founder and the first executive secretary of the American Society of Missiology. At present he is working to establish a new institution for world missions in Pasadena to be called the World Mission Center.